**Raising the Roof**

# RAISING THE ROOF

How to Solve the United Kingdom's Housing Crisis

## A collection of the 2018 Richard Koch Breakthrough Prize essays

EDITED AND WITH AN INTRODUCTORY ESSAY BY
JACOB REES-MOGG AND RADOMIR TYLECOTE

with contributions from

STEPHEN ASHMEAD · CALVIN CHAN
BEN CLEMENTS · LUKE MCWATTERS
DANIEL PYCOCK · THOMAS SCHAFFNER
CHARLES SHAW · GINTAS VILKELIS · WILLIAM WATTS

Institute of
**Economic** Affairs

First published in Great Britain in 2019 by
The Institute of Economic Affairs
2 Lord North Street
Westminster
London SW1P 3LB
in association with London Publishing Partnership Ltd
www.londonpublishingpartnership.co.uk

The mission of the Institute of Economic Affairs is to improve understanding of the fundamental institutions of a free society by analysing and expounding the role of markets in solving economic and social problems.

A CIP catalogue record for this book is available from the British Library.

ISBN 978-0-255-36782-0

Many IEA publications are translated into languages other than English or are reprinted. Permission to translate or to reprint should be sought from the Director General at the address above.

Typeset in Kepler by T&T Productions Ltd
www.tandtproductions.com

Printed and bound in Great Britain by Page Bros

# CONTENTS

## THE RICHARD KOCH BREAKTHROUGH PRIZE

The Institute of Economic Affairs launched the second Richard Koch Breakthrough Prize in order to find free-market solutions to the United Kingdom's housing crisis.

The First Prize was awarded to the best and boldest entry outlining a 'Free Market Breakthrough' policy to solve the UK housing crisis. Jacob Rees-Mogg MP was on the judging panel.

Competitors were asked to propose a single policy initiative which would:

- increase the number of houses built so as to markedly reduce the housing shortage in this country (this can be reduced through increased rental or ownership);
- increase the number and proportion of property owners in the UK;
- be politically possible.

Submissions were welcomed from individuals, groups of individuals, academia, the not-for-profit sector and all corporate bodies. There was also a Student Prize for which all students were eligible.

The prize pool consisted of £61,500, including a £50,000 grand prize for the winning entry.

Richard Koch – the benefactor and supporter of the prize – is a British author, speaker, investor, and a former management consultant and entrepreneur. He has written over twenty books on business and ideas, including *The 80/20 Principle*, about how to apply the Pareto principle in management and life.

*Raising the Roof* includes an introductory essay of the same title, first published as a separate IEA paper in July 2019, by Jacob Rees-Mogg and Radomir Tylecote.

The views in these essays are the private views of the authors and not of their employers. As with all IEA publications, the views expressed are also not those of the Institute (which has no corporate view), its managing trustees, Academic Advisory Council or other senior staff. The views in the Koch Prize essays outlined here should not necessarily be taken as the views of Jacob Rees-Mogg or Radomir Tylecote.

## Stephen Ashmead

Stephen Ashmead is currently a strategy and insight researcher for LiveWest, a housing association in southwest England. He has previously worked as a project coordinator in a small charity in Manchester working with Irish Travellers. He has a first-class honours degree in French Studies (University of London Institute in Paris) and a master's degree in Near and Middle Eastern Studies from the School of Oriental and African Studies. As well as the UK, he has lived in Paris, Spain and the Palestinian Territories.

## Calvin Chan

Calvin Chan is a graduate student in philosophy at Balliol College, Oxford. He received a bachelor's degree in the same subject from the University of Sydney and a master's degree from Brandeis University. Over the summer of 2018, he was an intern at the IEA.

## Ben Clements

Ben Clements works as an analyst for an intelligence firm in London and is responsible for helping clients to understand the business, political and security risks to their operations across the Asia-Pacific region. He graduated from the University of Manchester in 2016 with a degree in Chinese and Japanese. Ben was also a finalist in the Richard Koch Breakthrough Prize in 2017 and the IEA's Brexit Prize competition in 2014.

## Luke McWatters

Luke McWatters recently graduated from Camden School for Girls' Sixth Form with A-Levels in economics, history and maths. He is currently on a gap year completing his singing diploma and gaining economics-related work experience. He recently interned at Now-Casting, an econometrics firm, to further understand the technical side of economics. He will be reading Economics at university next year.

## Daniel Pycock

Daniel Pycock is a senior researcher to a Conservative MP in Parliament. Before that, he was a tax accountant in oil and gas and financial services for three years. Daniel was previously a finalist in the IEA's Brexit Prize competition in 2014. He graduated with an MA in history from the University of St Andrews and has a Graduate Diploma in economics from Birkbeck College, University of London.

## Jacob Rees-Mogg

Jacob Rees-Mogg is the Leader of the House of Commons and Conservative Member of Parliament for the constituency of North East Somerset. He was a member of the judging panel for the Richard Koch Breakthrough Prize, 2018. Jacob read History at Trinity College, Oxford, before co-founding Somerset Capital Management, an investment management firm that specialises in emerging markets.

## Thomas Schaffner

Thomas Schaffner is a Philosophy, Politics and Economics student at University College, Oxford, where he is the treasurer of his college's student committee. Out of term time, he works for the college's fundraising team as an Undergraduate Development Assistant. Growing up in Stroud, Gloucestershire, Tom was part of his local youth council.

## Charles Shaw

Charles Shaw is Data Manager at Ocean Media Group. He has a BSc in financial economics from Birkbeck, University of London, and is currently studying for a master's degree in financial risk management. Charles writes regularly on economics, finance and statistics.

## Radomir Tylecote

Dr Radomir Tylecote is Research Fellow at the Institute of Economic Affairs. He has an MPhil from Cambridge University and a PhD from Imperial College London Business School. Among other IEA publications he is the co-author of *Plan A+: Creating a Prosperous Post-Brexit UK* and *Freedom to Flourish: UK Regulatory Autonomy, Recognition, and a Productive Economy*. He is regularly published in the *Daily Telegraph*, *CityAM* and elsewhere.

## Gintas Vilkelis

Gintas Vilkelis is a technology entrepreneur. After working in physics for over twenty years, his current focus is on medical technology. He is the founder of a start-up that will bring faster and more accurate diagnostics to patients. Growing up in Soviet-occupied Lithuania made Gintas passionate about making sure that Marxism doesn't gain a firm foothold in the West.

## William Watts

William Watts is reading Philosophy, Politics and Economics at Jesus College, Oxford. In 2018, he graduated from City of London School and undertook a gap year in which he worked as a private tutor and on a research project investigating digital transformation across a range of industries in the Chinese economy.

## FIGURES

# PART ONE

# RAISING THE ROOF

# 1 RAISING THE ROOF[1]

Jacob Rees-Mogg and Radomir Tylecote

## Summary

- The United Kingdom's housing costs are now among the highest on earth, the economic and social impacts severe. Since 1970, the average price of a house has risen four-and-a-half-fold after inflation. No other OECD country has experienced a price increase of this magnitude over this period. London is virtually the most expensive major city in the world for renting or buying a home (per square foot). People often avoid moving to work in productive sectors because nearby housing is too expensive. The proportion of Britons who need financial support for housing is almost unique.
- The 1947 Town and Country Planning Act put land use under unprecedented statutory control, and the resulting regulation has caused at least half the rise

---

1 This essay was originally published as a separate paper in July 2019. The authors are particularly grateful for the advice of John Myers of London Yimby, Nicholas Boys Smith at Create Streets, Robert Wickham and Keith Boyfield, as well as the Koch Prize–winning authors, many of whose ideas have contributed to this essay.

in house prices over the last generation. The 'green belts' the Act created have grown far beyond what was planned, more than doubling in size since the 1970s, taking in derelict and already developed land, leading to building on more attractive areas. The complex and bureaucratic planning system has favoured big housebuilding corporations over small builders. The resulting identikit estates have helped drive Nimbyism.

- Since the war, government has also centralised taxation. With 95 per cent of tax collected centrally, local authorities have little incentive to allow housebuilding in order to gain additional revenue from new residents.
- National-level taxes drive house prices higher: Stamp Duty hinders downsizing; tax on buy-to-let landlords increases rents; 'Help to Buy' has made it harder to buy, inflating demand and pushing up prices.
- Central government control over the housing market was intended to provide homes, preserve an attractive environment and enhance our cities. It has failed on every count. Radical action is needed to lower housing costs. This means allowing more homes to be built by removing fiscal and regulatory barriers that hinder supply.
- Tax distortions at national level should be reversed; then government can begin the process of tax devolution. For example, Stamp Duty could be cut to 2010 levels, simplified, and then devolved to local government; non-property Inheritance Tax should be cut to the level of property, and Capital Gains Tax

reduced on shares; discrimination against buy-to-let landlords should be ended.

- More government land can be used for housing. Reverse Compulsory Purchase Orders – effectively a new Right to Buy – would allow the private sector to demand its sale. In addition, a cabinet minister could be given responsibility for identifying and releasing state land.

- Where green belt land achieves none of its official purposes, it can be selectively reclassified, with a presumed right to development. Most green belt land should remain, however. This proposal should apply in particular to derelict or already developed sites. Green belt land near transport hubs should be a declassification priority, including Metropolitan Green Belt land within realistic walking distance of a railway station. The amount of green belt land needed is very small: just 3.9 per cent of London's green belt is needed for one million homes.

- Permitted development rights for individual streets (in cities) or villages would see residents *gain* from building, as controlling local building lets people demand the styles that research shows they want (instead of tower blocks, for example). Residents of individual streets should have the right to vote to 'extend or replace' permitted development rights (for example by increasing the height of houses), subject to a design code they select. Letting urban streets densify *and* beautify will remove much public opposition to expanding the housing stock.

- Urban local authorities should allow light-touch 'notification' to give self-builds fast-track planning permission. Residents would build according to a style guide if one were applied by a local authority or street. Style guides created the beauty of Bath and Bloomsbury. There is no reason not to use them once more. No one has a monopoly on beauty, however. Style guides should be optional.

## Introduction

It is no coincidence that the United Kingdom has both the most centralised planning system of any large country in the democratic world, and one of the worst housing crises in the democratic world. Quite simply, the central planning of housebuilding does not work.

Our country's attempt to place housebuilding considerably under central state control since World War II, however well-intentioned, is, paradoxically, why the centre demands housebuilding and does not get it; it is why, when housing is built, it is so often disliked, leading to the Nimbyism that so befuddles Whitehall; and it is why, despite the business of housebuilding being so profitable, houses still go unbuilt. We build too few houses, which are too small, which people do not like, and which are in the wrong places.

This paper will describe a radical programme to cut the Gordian Knot that is our centralised planning system. When this is put into action, some of which can be done incrementally, the United Kingdom will be able to undo its almost uniquely severe housing crisis.

At first glance, our central proposition may seem counter-intuitive. Surely the central state is exactly the organisation that can 'push through' new housebuilding. In fact, since the end of World War II, by centralising almost all taxation and much decision-making from our local governments and localities – to a degree seen elsewhere only in socialist countries – it has thwarted the free market which could otherwise build the houses people actually want. Here, a socialist system has meant the usual socialist outcome: failure. Central government is responsible for most of the United Kingdom's housing crisis.

We will discuss below how this came about after 1945, and how it can be solved. Before that, it is important to understand how serious our problem now is.

Our failure to build is often called our most serious economic problem. The evidence tells us that it is, in fact, a catastrophe. For over a generation, we have built houses at a lower rate than any other country with comparable data. Estimates suggest a shortfall below the desirable level of new-build housing of 2.5 million since 1992 (Cheshire 2018); since 1970, the average price of a house has risen four-and-a-half-fold after inflation, where the UK is again an outlier, with no other OECD country experiencing a price increase of this magnitude over the period (Niemietz 2016). In the 1970s, the average buyer needed under three gross annual salaries for a house. Now, before interest payments, this is over seven, also making the UK unique.

The housing costs Britons face are now among the highest in world, and this holds for house prices or rents, in absolute terms or relative to income. There is a shortage of housing for first-time buyers, in the social housing sector, and in private accommodation (ibid.). We lack houses of every type.

**Figure 1    House prices in real terms, 1970–2012 (1970 = 100)**

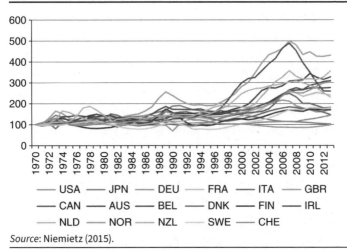

*Source*: Niemietz (2015).

The housing shortage is already a cause of inequality. We lack homes (among other buildings) near the best job markets especially. This is a particularly serious problem, because young people who would otherwise move to better jobs are often, understandably, simply not prepared to bear the costs of nearby housing, so those who would work in our most productive sectors choose less productive jobs elsewhere (Myers 2017). Britain's economy is needlessly held back.

This also means Britons are increasingly barred from their own capital city. London is now virtually the most expensive major city in the world for renting or buying a home (per square foot), although other cities in the UK are also extremely expensive by world standards. The impact of house prices on demand for housing benefit is also sadly predictable, with the proportion of our people needing financial support for housing costs almost unique among comparable countries, and the average cost of housing benefit now over £900 a year per household (Meakin 2015).

**Figure 2    Proportion of the population receiving financial support for housing costs (housing benefit or equivalent), 2009 (per cent)**

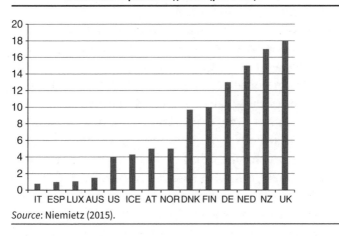

*Source*: Niemietz (2015).

The fact of the UK's failure to build housing is clear. It is therefore reasonable to ask how we arrived here.

## Causes: how we tied the Gordian Knot

The centrepiece of the British planning system is the Town and Country Planning Act, passed by Clement Attlee's government in 1947. Combined with the system of green belts that appeared in the 1950s as a result,[2] our planning system can now fairly be described as a series of amendments around the structure of this Act (see Boyfield and Wickham 2019). Naturally, planning and building regulations existed before 1947 (some long before: it has been illegal to roof with thatch in the City of London since the thirteenth century), but the Act effectively nationalised development rights in England and Wales (ibid.). As a result, land use and ownership are now subject to more statutory control than ever in our history.

Research strongly suggests that, despite much discussed factors that are very specific to localities (such as foreign resident demand in central London), at least half of the rise in house prices between 1974 and 2008 is due to regulatory constraints (Hilber and Vermeulen 2016), and a minimum 35 per cent of the average UK house price has arisen directly from planning constraints (the proportion is much higher in London and the southeast of England (ibid.), with local restrictiveness by percentage of applications refused now the most important source of house price variation (Cheshire 2018); much of this restrictiveness, as we will describe, results from central government action). This regulation has been especially effective at imposing highly unusual limits on *supply* (Cheshire 2009).

---

2   Although the earliest green belt designations appeared through the Green Belt (London and Home Counties) Act 1938, these were very small areas of land.

Like so much central government activity, in many ways this Act was well meant. Attlee's post-war government wanted to restrict urban sprawl, and believed the green belts the Act instructed local governments to designate would create 'circular parks' (Myers 2017) around our cities (green belts should not be confused with Areas of Outstanding Natural Beauty (AONBs), Sites of Special Scientific Interest (SSSIs) or National Parks, all separately protected). Green belt designation involves an almost total prohibition on development, even when a local community wants houses to be built. But the green belt has grown far beyond what was first proposed. Even in 1974, green belt only covered 692,800 hectares: by 2017 it had more than doubled to 1,634,700 hectares (ibid.). Green belt now constitutes 14 per cent of the land in England, but green belt classification does not account for the actual quality of the land, or whether an appropriate style of housing could beautify it and lead to local approval for building.

With such limits on supply, central government has at various times responded to the inevitable inability of local governments to build by taking more control unto itself and trying to force them to do so. The most direct example was John Prescott's 2004 Planning and Compulsory Purchase Act, which stripped local government of even more of its planning role (Jenkins 2004), taking rural conservation and economic development functions into the regional offices of his own department,[3] and saw

---

3  At the time the Office of the Deputy Prime Minister, now the Ministry for Housing, Communities and Local Government.

Whitehall officials determining 'Regional Spatial Strategies'. Though now broadly revoked, these covered such areas of planning as converting farmland to industrial use, new towns and village expansion, and individual district housing targets (naturally prepared by central government).

Among its other impacts, this lack of local control is a major reason UK local election turnout is below the European average. As Simon Jenkins has written (ibid.), this:

> stripped the English counties of democratic purpose... The proposed system was widely ridiculed. It was likened [to] Soviet social engineering (by *The Times*) and the death of rural England (by the Green Party). Mr Blair and Mr Prescott were unmoved. The 2004 Act imposed central targets on the local planning framework to a degree unknown in England and unheard of elsewhere in Europe. It marked the end of popular control over the evolution of the English landscape, control that ran from the Middle Ages through the Industrial Revolution to the end of the 20th century. It was a return to the ancient prerogative of 'the king's forests'. Central government was initiating a truly nationalised system of land use of a sort familiar only to communism.

Meanwhile, though scholars often highlight the fall in supply from 1950, Figure 3 is more compelling. Showing gross and net building, it outlines how government-driven estate construction in the 1960s also involved the large-scale demolition of existing homes, distorting the real picture.

The overall change in dwellings shows us the persistently low net level of housebuilding since 1947.

**Figure 3    Gross and net change in dwellings (as a
percentage of the existing dwelling stock),
England and Wales (1801–2016)**

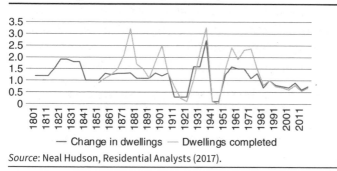

— Change in dwellings  — Dwellings completed

*Source*: Neal Hudson, Residential Analysts (2017).

Our failure to build enough houses since the 1940s is often called a market failure, but this is not true. It is a failure of state planning. The result is that not enough houses are being built, they are too small for contemporary needs, and, as we will discuss, they are frequently not the type or style of houses that people want to live in, or want to see built in their neighbourhoods.

## No skin in the game: local incentives and the homes people want

Having placed severe constraints on supply, during the same post-war period the British government made another change which is vital to understanding our problem: they took central control of tax.

The UK now has more centralised taxation than almost any other democratic country: having expanded to fight two successive world wars, with the arrival of peace, Whitehall found myriad ways to put its new-found supremacy to use, and resolved that central government needed fiscal control. Today, 95 per cent of our tax take goes to the central state (Wadsworth 2009), and, as Figure 4 illustrates, only much smaller countries are comparably centralised (in Canada, for example, this is more like 50 per cent).

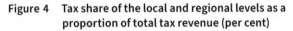

**Figure 4    Tax share of the local and regional levels as a proportion of total tax revenue (per cent)**

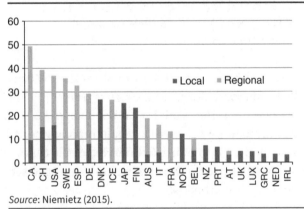

*Source*: Niemietz (2015).

Local authorities have seen their powers reduced accordingly, increasingly becoming little more than distributors of 'grants', or the money that Whitehall deigns to give back to them. This means that where development is not proscribed by green belt status anyway, a local authority that is considering allowing houses to be built knows that it will receive relatively little direct tax benefit from housing for new residents, but it will face some of the costs of the necessary new infrastructure, and the initial administrative burden. It is liable therefore to find itself disincentivised from allowing housebuilding.[4]

Conversely, a local authority that blocks all new housing will bear very little cost. The tax rises that will be needed to pay for the extra housing benefit (which results from the higher cost of housing) will be spread nationwide and back to the British taxpayer. Meanwhile, Whitehall is too distant from the level of the local community to feel the results of its actions (this is what Nassim Nicholas Taleb calls a lack of political 'skin in the game'). If central government had wanted to design a system that would drive up the cost of housing, it could hardly have done better.

When we look at our tax system on the national level, we see that it also leads to the less efficient allocation of housing. For instance, high nationwide Stamp Duty penalises property transactions, impedes downsizing, and harms labour mobility (in this case people's ability to move to the work they want to do), misallocating dwellings and causing a welfare loss. Whitehall has thrown in yet another distortion in our inheritance tax system, where in treating housing wealth preferentially to other wealth it has further inflated demand relative to supply (Niemietz 2016). But it gets worse.

---

4 Other aspects local governments may consider could include new voters with different political leanings, but this is beyond the scope of this paper. While the dynamics of taxation incentives are complex, the evidence points us to the importance of beginning fiscal decentralisation.

Next, by exempting many homes (but not shares) from Capital Gains Tax (CGT), government has driven up house prices further, by encouraging the misallocation of savings (Myers 2017). (Here we can add the high rate of VAT on restoration (HMRC 2018), which has helped disincentivise the reuse of cherished buildings for homes, causing them to fall into disrepair, which is both a loss in itself and has driven down supply still more.)

Next, tax on buy-to-let landlords. This was an attempt to boost the owner-occupied housing sector, but served as a fiscal strike on privately rented housing which also made landlords scapegoats for the housing crisis (Beck and Booth 2019). A classic example of government trying to compensate for previous mistakes by making some more (while benefiting no one but itself), this is also likely to have pushed up rents (with a tiny benefit to buyers which is limited to the already wealthy) (ibid.).

Next, according to the homelessness charity Shelter, 'Help to Buy' has driven house prices even higher, by over £8,000 (so far) (Van Lohuizen 2015), because the policy inflated demand, which in any market with inelastic supply is liable to raise prices (Niemietz 2016). This is also self-defeating, and another policy that has made the housing crisis worse.

These government initiatives and 'big push' tactics all have one thing in common: they do not work. In broad terms, they fail because they attempt to treat the symptoms but fail to treat the cause. In this way they are very much like the Whitehall approach to Nimbyism.

## *Nimbyism: more symptom than cause*

The results, on a national scale, of the inability of local governments and areas to benefit from housebuilding have been more profound than is usually understood. As we have seen, many people are unable to move where they want to work, others are forced to leave their own towns as they become too expensive. But that the incentives are to block, not approve, new homes, combined with the inability of neighbourhoods and villages to determine what kind of houses they see built, has helped cause adversarial planning processes of great length and cost.[5] Added to the costs of tax on building in general, this means that, increasingly, only large incumbent housebuilders can make a profit, especially because a developer may need to have numerous planning applications in progress simultaneously for one to succeed.

The price of these combined planning applications must then be combined with the price of land, which means smaller developers are priced out, and that there is little margin left over for arguably the most important thing of all: the design of homes. The result has been the estates of identikit housing that have sprung up across the land, at the expense of both smaller and more local developers, as well as those companies willing to spend more on the housing designs that people actually want, including locally fitting architecture. This means it is frequently

---

5   The length of these processes, and the apparent increase in length of time required, are discussed for example in Ball (2008).

impossible to build the kind of houses that would reduce opposition to building itself. (As Pennington (2002) has described, in economic terms this means housebuilding has become a special interest issue, whereby a small group captures a too-large benefit while imposing a larger cost on a larger group, while benefiting from a political process skewed in its favour.[6])

We have thus arrived at the economic and cultural conundrum that explains why we have become unable to build the houses that people want to live in. And it is hard to deny that much of the resistance to housebuilding, and to building in general, arises because of how people expect a new building will look.

As we look at how to cut the knot, it is worth asking how this part of the problem occurred. Leaving the political question temporarily aside, it is important to recall that economics is also a field of moral sentiments. We often call these 'values', or the shared understandings of what constitutes good behaviour. For example, Britain developed first, not because of some fluke, but because our values placed a relatively strong emphasis on private property rights and freedom under the rule of law (amongst other things), and these helped people invent freely, profit from their own innovations and hard work, and reinvest without fear of being fleeced. So markets function best when the actors within them behave according to the values shared by the other participants. When one group of participants fails to trust the other, however, they are more likely to demand

---

6    According to public choice theory.

costly protections against bad behaviour, meaning burdensome regulations or outright bans, harming growth.

So it may also be no coincidence that the explosion, since the 1960s especially, of controls and bans on building has been accompanied by a popular loss of confidence that architects will build things people want to look at: in other words that they will share their values. Indeed, a large body of research now demonstrates precisely this.

In one experiment, volunteers were shown photographs of unfamiliar people and buildings, then asked to rate their attractiveness. One group of volunteers were architects, the other was not. The groups were in harmonious agreement about people's attractiveness, but non-architects and architects had strikingly different opinions on what constituted an attractive building (Boys-Smith 2018), a disagreement that became more pronounced with experience, as if architects were being taught to dislike the very things the public found beautiful. And in recent opinion polls, when asked what they wanted from new homes, 74 per cent of people said their home should fit its surroundings, while only 11 per cent wanted a home to be modern even if it did not (Airey et al. 2018). Today, 65 per cent think traditionally designed housing helps good relations in a community (ibid.).

But many architects seem determined to maintain this great divide. Royal Institute of British Architects (RIBA) prizes demand evidence of sustainability, but none of what the public actually think of a building (Boys-Smith 2018). Indeed, when asked recently why the council he worked for had chosen for housing an incoherent jumble of glass and steel towers instead of buildings local people wanted, one planner replied that the latter would win them no prizes from RIBA (one duly arrived). We seem to know this instinctively: when a traditional building appears, the joke goes, nobody likes it except the public.

So the evidence tells us that architecture has diverged from public wants. But how might this divergence have come about? A cultural trend was clearly at work in the twentieth century, and some architecture has been so unpopular that local communities have taken to the streets to prevent its construction. When we compare, at the extremes, the line and elegance of the Georgian Square (which the rich are free to choose) with brutalist estates like the now largely demolished Robin Hood Gardens (which the poor had forced upon them), we understand the development of strict rules, and frequently simply bans, to control and prevent building. We also understand that much-maligned thing, Nimbyism.

Here, the public are accused of behaving irrationally, claiming to want housebuilding nationally while attempting to block it in their own neighbourhoods. This is not irrational, however. If you know the houses being planned on the field next door will do genuine harm to your town or village, depriving it of local character, and you also know that future potential residents will agree, which will harm the value of the home in which you have invested much of your salary, you will be right to try to stop this building (note, however, that many homeowners do not even seek to maintain high prices, and oppose building simply for aesthetic reasons). You may oppose building even as you regret it, because you know that houses need to be built (Pennington 2002), perhaps for your own children.

It is too easy, then, to criticise Nimbyism, which is a symptom, not cause, of our problems. But what if the market could induce the return of loved buildings, of widely accepted architectural beauty? Then many of the interventions in this market, in which values have diverged and trust has faltered, would be rendered unnecessary.

The good news is that it can.

The centralisation of tax and planning processes that promote the types of buildings that people do not want: we can undo this. The inflation of prices through the excessive use of green belt classification, even for low-quality land where people want houses to be built, has done the same: this too can be undone. The capacity for householders and communities to elect, for example, their own style of building, has been hindered by self-defeating control: this we can also change.

Whitehall's taking control of housebuilding created and exacerbated the very housing crisis it intended to manage, harming our national beauty and pitting government against people along the way. In the two decades from the late 1950s, having chronically restricted supply, government planners also directly imposed their preferred types of housing on the British people, giving us some of the most disliked housing we have seen. Now, the tower block became a very symbol of the belief that the planner knows best. In modern Britain, there are few better examples of why markets and choice work better than state planning, and of the cruelty that results from our failure to observe this.

The historian David Kynaston has recounted how, in 1958, as fifteen new blocks were imposed on a square mile of Bethnal Green alone, a newspaper correspondent walked among the rubble of the razed streets, and saw on the remaining scraps of brickwork a silent protest: 'again and again someone had chalked on the shattered walls "I lived here"' (Kynaston 2015).

In Birmingham, as mass relocation to tower blocks gathered pace (from housing which had clearly needed improvement), the chairman of the city council's Planning Subcommittee decided that 'it is understandable that people cling to the old idea of things [but] we shall overcome this prejudice'. In Sheffield, a Marxist sociologist decided that 'the success of the new tall blocks suggests that the traditional attitude is not permanent' (ibid.: 48–49).

Just as the evidence of the harm tower blocks were doing became unignorable in the 1960s, devotion to them in government became unstoppable. Mass petitions against these buildings, such as from 11,500 citizens in Bristol, were ignored. When a BBC programme in 1961 investigated the growing incidence of depression among the out-of-town high-rise estates to which communities had been uprooted, one architects' journal responded with irritation at local people's opinions having even been asked: 'good scripting and good camerawork could say far more about architecture than any amount of interviewing of tenants', while one GP complained of the 'excessive demands for his services' among residents. A correspondent noted breezily: 'There are, of course, social objections to compelling families with young children to live in high flats', but this was not allowed to intrude on 'integral plans' (ibid.: 49).

On the rare occasions when their opinions were asked, people were massively against the new tower blocks, and wanted their own houses. In a 1962 opinion poll in Leeds among people whose houses were to be cleared, only five per cent wanted high-rise flats, which they were inevitably given. Another newspaper report, 'The Sky Prisoners', surveyed 62 new blocks in the London area, and found that 52 per cent of two- to five-year-olds played only inside the flat. One mother despaired that her child could not go out to play because they were high up and near a main road. Even though she was at home, 'in desperation ... I have put him in a nursery and now feel I am missing the best years of his life'. In Oldham, one member of the Housing Committee stated: 'I know that many people do not like flats, but ... the sooner [they are] accepted by the townspeople, the happier they will be about it' (ibid.: 672–73).

The housing consultant Elizabeth Denby had 'plenty [of] evidence to show that [people] really wanted the type of building they had before ... a house and garden'. She also found in her analysis of four London squares that 'family houses with a reasonably large common garden and good private gardens can be grouped at the same density as family flats, costing less and giving greater satisfaction'. Whereas tower blocks were an approach 'in which architects delight', she had 'yet to find one who lives in such a block himself' (ibid.: 48). The evidence was simply dismissed.

State control over building, like much else, divides society into a 'who' and a 'whom'. Socialist ways of doing things tend to mean power for the planner and penury for the planned-for: the state's imposition of ugliness and isolation on the British households who, in the twentieth century, lacked a choice about where they could live was no exception. But we believe that the best vehicle to provide beautiful and well-liked homes for all is choice. Just as a relatively free market in advanced technologies has made these available to virtually everyone in our country, a free market in beauty can mean the same for homes that people will want to see built.

It is also certainly time to be more assertive about beauty itself. We can propose one way: *take back pastiche.* For too long, 'pastiche' has been a term of abuse. No longer. The truth is that all good building is pastiche: Inigo Jones reinvented Vitruvian symmetry to create a (very inaccurate) pastiche of classical temple architecture.[7] In turn, the Palace of Westminster is a Victorian pastiche of Medieval Gothic. Within a few years, no one remembers that a building was pastiche. It is simply enjoyed for its beauty.

But by freeing the market (while maintaining the necessary rules on building safety), the housing that people find fitting will appear organically anyway. When we describe

---

7   A Roman, Marcus Vitruvius Pollio, established Vitruvian proportions in *De Architectura* in 30–15 BC. The book was itself a pastiche of the architectural concepts of the Greek Golden Age around four centuries earlier. It was rediscovered in a Swiss monastery by the Florentine Poggio Bracciolini in 1414, before the English translation that inspired Inigo Jones appeared in 1547. All style is pastiche.

the rejuvenation of a free market for building, we describe the capacity of freedom itself to generate beauty, and then of beauty to regenerate support for building, or more freedom: one virtue will sustain another.

Therefore, to solve the problem, we should clearly understand the Gordian Knot, which in summary looks like this:

- The central state took control of taxation and denied local governments the incentives to allow more houses to be built, generally leaving them only the costs.
- It then asked many of them to prevent any housebuilding on large areas of land called green belt.
- Planning processes locally then became so difficult that big incumbent housebuilders took advantage, leading to indentikit housing estates across the country.
- Nimbyism grew, making housebuilding harder still.
- Whitehall then decided Nimbyism itself was the problem, vowing to 'push through' housebuilding, which has caused more resistance, while all the time a free market could be building the houses we need.

## Solutions

The outcome we need is relatively straightforward. We need to build many more houses, but without causing the value of people's homes themselves to fall,[8] instead aiming

---

8   It is important to avoid negative equity for many reasons, not least its implications for the stability of the financial system.

for a gradual stabilisation of prices nearer the normal multiple of three times earnings. This means rolling out a programme of reform incrementally, demonstrating in one or two major cities first, for example, that the reforms are both beneficial and will not lead to negative equity (meanwhile, although fixed-rate mortgages have become more popular, it is important to remember that interest rates closer to normal levels would see many homeowners' repayments become more demanding).

That the current system has been so detrimental does not mean a choice between continuity and no restraint at all, however. Individual and voter preference means that local governments and communities will continue to impose restraints on building, in terms of both place and style. The need, then, is to change the centripetal dynamics of a system that simply does not achieve the necessary outcomes. The solutions proposed here would, incrementally, reform our failing system of central planning for housebuilding.

## Cutting tax, decentralising tax

Fiscal decentralisation is an important part of the solution. The centralisation of our property taxes deprives local government of incentives to allow building or to ensure the quality of the environment, while the structure of fiscal incentives at the national level badly distorts our housing market.

The solutions begin at the national level itself, where seeking more homeownership does not justify attempting artificially to inflate it by creating tax burdens elsewhere, such as Capital Gains Tax (CGT) on shares, that leave homes exempt. This simply increases house prices, and this distortion can be reduced by lowering CGT on shares (Wadsworth 2009).

High Stamp Duty also harms people's ability to move and to buy. As James Mirrlees described it, this tax '[defies] the most basic of economic principles by taxing transactions and produced inputs respectively' (Beck and Booth 2019). Stamp Duty can therefore be reduced to 2010 levels, then devolved so that local governments have the capacity to reduce it further (though not to increase it back above 2010 levels). As we have seen, VAT on maintenance and restoration also harms supply, and can be abolished (see Meakin 2016).

Stamp Duty is also too complex, with lower rates for self-built homes and properties left empty or allowed to become derelict,[9] creating an incentive for people to leave properties vacant. The latter harms supply and the capacity to move, while making it difficult for buyers to pay the right tax (although the first-time buyer exemption, which does help people to buy, should remain).

Meanwhile, as Beck and Booth (ibid.) have proposed, investment in property should be treated like investment in any other business, with all business costs deducted before taxable income is determined, and with no discrimination between different vehicles for holding property.

---

9   Following a recent tribunal ruling: https://www.smithcooper.co.uk/news -insights/a-win-for-developers-tribunal-rules-dilapidated-and-derelict -houses-are-not-liable-for-stamp-duty-surcharges/

It is also important to consider the role of brownfield site redevelopment. Some caveats are important here. The redevelopment of some of this land into housing would be economically feasible only with subsidy, which we do not propose. Furthermore, many post-industrial brownfield sites are found in areas of the Midlands and North East especially, where there is less demand for housing. However, a better tax system can still help housebuilding on brownfield sites. Corporation tax relief is supposed to be available to clean up contaminated and derelict land, but the small print deters investors, with considerable detail on what can and cannot be claimed. Meanwhile, tax relief is only obtainable on profits, but the cost is paid at the construction stage, before any profits appear against which to claim relief. These are obvious areas for reform (Haslehurst 2014).

Beginning with a degree of fiscal devolution would see local authorities rewarded for cutting Stamp Duty (thus easing a restriction on supply) by attracting more residents to become net contributors to local budgets, so blocking development would have a greater cost (ibid.).

Local governments would also be rewarded by being able to keep the revenue they generate when they allow housebuilding: more houses would then mean more residents and more council tax–take, for instance.

It is important to achieve proof of concept first, through an incremental approach that could begin, for example, in Birmingham and Manchester, generating support for a nationwide roll-out.

## *A new Right to Buy: reverse compulsory purchase orders*

We have seen how the scale of the green belt creates serious problems for supply, and we return to this below. Another constraint on supply is that 6 per cent of land in England and Wales (about 900,000 hectares) remains in direct state ownership. This vast land holding includes 170,000 hectares of Ministry of Defence land (itself over 1 per cent of the land area of England and Wales), while NHS Property Services and NHS Trusts also own at least 4,500 hectares (Boyfield and Wickham 2019).

Among urban local authorities, where demand for housing is often most severe, 15 per cent of land is owned by the public sector (ibid.). In eight local authorities (Brighton and Hove, Barking and Dagenham, Eastbourne, Rushmoor (comprising Aldershot and Farnborough), Gosport, Leicester, Portsmouth and Stevenage) the public sector owns over 40 per cent of all land (ibid.), an extraordinary figure.

Yet progress on land disposals has been slow. According to a National Audit Office study of the public land sold from 2011 to 2015, only 200 new homes had been completed on a sample of sites with the capacity for 8,600 homes, suggesting that housebuilding is far below the overall capacity of 109,500 homes from all these sites (NAO 2016). The government target is now to sell land for the construction of 320,000 homes by 2020, which currently appears very optimistic.

There are obvious ways to change this. It is important to be radical in order to build houses on these great tracts of land, transforming the Right to Buy to apply to government land; a mechanism to allow people the right to demand the sale of government land is needed, without which progress is liable to be slow. Government can also reverse the compulsory purchase procedures it has used to acquire land, using Disposal Orders for public sector land to create entrepreneurial opportunity: compulsory purchase orders in reverse.

As Boyfield and Wickham (2019) propose, the Government Property Unit in the Cabinet Office can accelerate the Government Estate Strategy, which has sold little public land so far, with a senior cabinet minister made responsible for identifying and releasing public land for housing[10] (we can also review whether the £45 million given to the Local Authority Land Release Fund has been good value for money (ibid.)). Small housebuilders, who are also vital for these sites, would also benefit from exemption from Community Infrastructure Levy (CIL) and Section 106 payments (except for safety) (ibid.). There is also an argument that this land should be sold off at land value, not building value. Importantly, unlike for brownfield sites, much of this land is in high-demand areas, such as in the southeast of England.

---

10  This is also recommended by the House of Lords Select Committee on Economic Affairs (2016).

## *Making the green belt do its job*

Sadly, the very language we use about housing now suggests central command: housing must be 'driven through', or 'forced upon' a locality, as if we were describing a patient who does not know what is good for him. As we have seen, this is the result of a half century in which the British people have learned that new housing will lack a sense of place. It need not be this way.

The green belt has expanded well beyond what was originally intended. Some Metropolitan (London) Green Belt land is now twenty miles from a London borough (ibid.). Local authorities can already 'amend' their local green belt (Myers 2017), but if a local authority has decreed that the green belt boundary is a 'strategic policy', which they often do, this will simply not happen.

It is also important to remember that development on greenfield sites other than green belt is more harmful to the environment and to people's wellbeing (Papworth 2016), but this 'green belt hopping' into rural areas beyond the green belt is precisely what is taking place, and failure to reform the green belt will exacerbate this. Selective green belt reclassification nationwide is therefore necessary. The purpose, however, is not the complete scrapping of the green belt, which is unnecessary. Most green belt would remain; that which is declassified can, through appropriate housebuilding, become *more* attractive.

The green belt is too big, and it often fails to achieve its purpose of aesthetic and environmental preservation. But it has served *some* purpose, in preventing the growth of huge conurbations at the expense of individual character: we do not intend for Bath to become a southeastern suburb of Bristol, for example, nor should the larger city devour the Somerset countryside on its southern flank.[11] By the same token, the green belt preservation of Sheffield's Pennine river valleys clearly serves an environmental purpose. Re-classification would not remove all green belt designation.

The National Planning Policy Framework (NPPF)[12] states that the green belt has five functions:

1. Checking the unrestricted sprawl of large built-up areas.
2. Preventing neighbouring towns merging into one another.
3. Helping safeguard the countryside from encroachment.
4. Preserving the setting and special character of historic towns.
5. Helping urban regeneration, by encouraging the recycling of derelict and other urban land.

Therefore, areas of green belt that do not support a single one of the five NPPF purposes may be declassified.[13] This

11 For a deeper discussion of the economic and philosophical questions raised by the green belt, see Pennington (2002).

12 https://assets.publishing.service.gov.uk/government/uploads/system/uploads/attachment_data/file/807247/NPPF_Feb_2019_revised.pdf

13 We acknowledge that it may be argued that green belt land always fulfils function 5; however, our emphasis here is on derelict land within the green belt, and the tendency of wrongly classified green belt land to cause green belt hopping instead of urban regeneration.

would include green belt land that has already been developed: in many such cases, continued green belt classification prevents beautification, and many examples illustrate how ongoing green belt designation is actually preventing the maintenance of an attractive environment.

**Figure 5  An example map of a green belt location**

*Source*: Papworth (2016).

Figure 5 shows one example in Essex, a slither of farmland between Theydon Bois station on London Underground's Central Line and the M25–M11 junction, where green belt designation is preventing housebuilding to very limited environmental or aesthetic benefit. Meanwhile, Figure 6 shows that green belt land does not always prevent urban sprawl.

The photographs in Figure 7 are examples of poorly selected green belt land, and demonstrate how classification often fails in its objectives of environmental and aesthetic protection.

## Figure 6 Green belt land in the London Borough of Redbridge

*Source*: Papworth (2016).

This means that for reclassification (or 'rezoning') to work, central government will need to categorise where green belt land has become low quality. This implies initial central activity to help free a local market, but where green belt has not succeeded in its aim of environmental and aesthetic preservation, it is logical that it can be declassified. The majority of the green belt will remain, and will still be able to prevent disliked urban sprawl.

Releasing green belt land near transport hubs would also be a priority. This would include Metropolitan Green Belt land within realistic walking distance of a railway station (Papworth 2016). Even excluding locations with other protective designations, meaning places with genuine environmental value, there are approximately 20,000 hectares of green belt land within 800 metres of a station (ibid.; Meakin 2015). At current density levels of 50 houses per hectare, 20,000 hectares on greenfield sites within the outer circuit of the Metropolitan Green Belt (with 400,000 homes assumed to be within Greater London) would mean space for almost one million homes (ibid.).

**Figure 7    Examples of poorly selected green belt land**

*Source*: McDonagh (2018).

It is therefore untrue to claim that declassifying some green belt means the widespread 'concreting over' of greenfield sites.[14] In total, the Metropolitan Green Belt covers over 514,000 hectares, four times the built-on urban area of London. Building one million homes on green belt land would mean developing merely 3.9 per cent of this Metropolitan Green Belt land (with a presumed half as much again becoming private gardens) (Papworth 2016).

Green belt land that is already built on, that has been allowed to become derelict, and other brownfield areas within green belt, would also be declassified. While this housing could in theory be built on non–green belt greenfield sites, for example, this would be more harmful to the environment. For example, of 'metropolitan greenfield' land, 35,180 hectares are green belt, with the other 25,000 hectares classified as Metropolitan Open Land (with the same protection as Metropolitan Green Belt), or parkland and other areas, which are much more frequently used by local people (ibid.). Using (some) green belt land will in fact preserve the most cherished places. In the declassified zones of former green belt, there would be a presumed right to development.

This means that communities could in fact 'green' their green belts by developing the sections which have been allowed to become less attractive. It is this capacity for communities to select housing that blends in that will allow more houses to be built in the long run (unlike imposing

---

14  Cheshire (2014) states that 50 houses per hectare is 'the current norm'. For comparison, new London developments mainly in the inner city had an average density of 120 per hectare in 2012/13. See Papworth (2016).

the high-density tower blocks which create more resistance later). We will next discuss mechanisms to allow this to happen. This reform of the green belt would, we propose, begin with London, as well as Birmingham and Manchester. Gradualism is vital to demonstrate the benefits of these reforms.

## Choice not bureaucracy: freeing the market in beauty

Granting permitted development rights to individual streets or villages (the former in cities, the latter in rural areas) to 'build and beautify' would mean residents could *gain* from local building, by placing control over this construction with actual communities. This would give back the advantage to small developers, working as they can at the community level, or, in villages, the parish level.

In cities, this is a vital part of increasing urban density, but in desirable ways, for an urbanism rooted in freedom. However, like other local governments, London's Mayor cannot yet grant individual streets or communities control over housebuilding, which as John Myers of London Yimby has discussed, would need to change.

The need is clearly there. Swathes of our cities consist of two-storey houses built over the last hundred years; half of London homes are in buildings of one to two floors. Extending these upwards – or replacing them, with the support of a community, to create more homes – could increase dwelling space in a suburban street *fivefold* (ibid.). Let individual streets decide to award themselves the right to extend or replace homes and, over time, we can see five million more homes in the capital alone (ibid.). This would require individual streets being given the right to vote to give themselves permitted development rights to build upwards up to, for example, six storeys. Like other reforms that we describe, this would help end the big developers' virtual cartel.

The law can therefore be amended so that any residential city street could give itself additional development rights to 'extend or replace' up to a permissible height (with voting limited to absolute majorities of residents who have lived there beyond a certain time) (ibid.).[15] Meanwhile, designations such as Areas of Special Residential Character would remain, and not all streets will vote for these rights, simply where residents perceive more certain improvements.

There is little need to fear that residents would simply block development, however. When residents are asked whether every household on their street should be able to build upwards (by one to two floors), they are very often in favour (Airey et al. 2018). Aside from the incentive for residents who would gain from the increased value of larger properties, developers are perfectly capable of meeting local style needs when they too have the incentive. Devolving this power all the way to communities has the added benefit of cutting council costs and tax, and letting developers devote less resource to planning departments, more to the extra cost of good design (see Evans 1988).

---

15 The limits on height would help prevent excessive spillover effects, such as loss of light, overlooking or congestion.

This local control over building, including upwards, can solve much of our housing problem in cities. London on average has half as many homes per square mile as Kensington and Chelsea or Westminster, two of the boroughs considered most attractive.

When streets and villages can choose precisely this building, we will find much public opposition unlocked. Streets of suburban semis could, when owners wish, become denser streets of attractive mansion blocks or terraces, with a dramatic increase in square footage and value for the average suburban street into the bargain. Because in our cities, we already know how to build higher-density housing that people want to live in. The elegant proportions of Georgian terraces in these boroughs make them the most loved homes in London. They were also built at speed and volume (Terry 2018), precisely what is needed now.

No one has a monopoly on beauty, however. The more *dirigiste* approach would be to mandate that local authorities have a design and style guide. These should be optional, for local authorities, or for streets and villages. Some boroughs and other authorities will choose them, some will not, just as some streets will vote for them. When local governments set design codes in the past, the result was the construction of some of our finest cities, such as Bath, while London also had a number of codes before the twentieth century, such as in Bloomsbury. But it is important to note, like Stephen Davies, that 'the urban growth of [Victorian Britain] was voluntary and owed nothing to state plans ... It was driven by private initiative and speculation, directed by property rights ... the outcome was a process of urbanisation that was orderly but unplanned' (Davies 2002). The point is that, with the right local incentives (and rules on the safety and good condition of houses), there is no reason we cannot build cherished buildings once again.

Self-build would probably only be a relatively small part of the greater project of reform. Nonetheless, given individual owners' relative difficulty in negotiating planning processes, planning permission for self-builds could be fast-tracked, with a light-touch 'notification' process and with the presumption that people can build their own homes, under a style guide where a local authority agrees one (with local authorities given time to decide on one before new rules are brought in). We call this BIY: Build It Yourself.

Our failure to build houses is therefore a problem the market mechanism can solve. We do not need to *mandate* better building. That this is what the public want means that, if allowed to, the market will provide. The reforms we outline will bring down the cost of planning and increase the number of providers. This will increase competition, given the need to spend less before receiving planning approval. A less restrictive market will mean better building, and better building will itself reduce restrictiveness.

Cutting the Gordian Knot might therefore be done as follows:

- Devolving some taxation would benefit local property markets.

- Declassifying non-functioning areas of the green belt would release some of the most severe constraints on supply.
- Allowing still more local devolution of some planning powers, such as to the street and village level, would give the advantage back to smaller firms of builders and architects.
- This freedom will mean more houses, and houses that people want to live in and among.
- This will reduce resistance to housebuilding generally, rejuvenating productivity, home-ownership and our property-owning democracy itself.

## The beauty of freedom

This essay describes how replacing market freedom and local decision-making with central planning has caused the national crisis that is our failure to build houses, and how reforming this system, in a staged and steady manner, will undo this. We have set out what we believe can be done at this stage: we have not outlined every possible reform or devolution that may take place in due course. And while this is a free-market agenda that returns power to the locality, some central direction will be needed, in the first instance, to return it. Naturally, we also acknowledge that some scholars and decision-makers cleave to the central planning of housebuilding for understandable reasons: central government is clearly not incapable of building at all times. Hayek (1945), however, should perhaps have the last word on why decisions should not be with the central planner, whose knowledge can so often be illusory:

> [The] knowledge of the circumstances of which we must make use never exists in concentrated or integrated form but solely as the dispersed bits of incomplete and frequently contradictory knowledge which all the separate individuals possess. The economic problem of society is thus not merely a problem of how to allocate 'given' resources — if 'given' is taken to mean given to a single mind which deliberately solves the problem set by these 'data.' It is rather a problem of how to secure the best use of resources known to any of the members of society, for ends whose relative importance only these individuals know. Or, to put it briefly, it is a problem of the utilization of knowledge which is not given to anyone in its totality.

Much of our country's finest housing was created before the late 1940s, when the government took control. When it did, the housebuilding that research shows people find attractive – those Georgian terraces and Edwardian mansion blocks, for instance – ground almost to a halt. Now, the British people should be able to expect homes that they will want to live in.

The moral case for action is manifold. It is a great irony that our crisis was created by the over-mighty state behaving in socialist ways, but that its results are fuelling support for more socialist-inspired policies, such as rent controls and subsidy, which will only make the problem worse. These will lead to another generation of renters, prevented from joining our property-owning democracy. Our failure to build is already harming our children and grandchildren. Instead, like the homeownership project of the 1980s, radical action to build houses and increase homeownership is needed once more. We propose that the programme we have outlined will do much to solve the great national challenge of our times.

## Appendix: Outline of the current planning system

The following outline describes the general structure of the planning system (some elements refer to England especially).

First, the local planning authority depends on the form of local government. Many places have three local government tiers: county councils; district, borough or city councils; and parish or town councils (DCLG 2015). District councils deal with most planning matters (although areas such as transport are usually county council responsibilities), but where single-tier authorities exist these are responsible for the planning issues otherwise dealt with by districts and counties. In London the Mayor is responsible for some strategic planning applications (while in National Parks the park authority has planning responsibilities).

Local councillors' role depends on whether they are members of the decision-making planning committee; the local planning authority also appoints planning officers, who make around 90 per cent of decisions on planning applications. Decisions over larger developments are typically made by the planning committee, with officers making recommendations. Local authorities also provide planning enforcement services.

**Figure 8    General structure of the planning system**

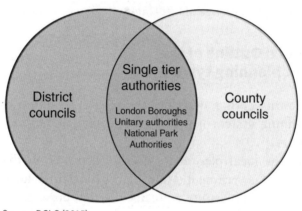

District
councils

Single tier
authorities

London Boroughs
Unitary authorities
National Park
Authorities

County
councils

*Source*: DCLG (2015).

Where parish and town councils still exist, they may comment on planning applications and participate in producing Neighbourhood Plans (below), but otherwise have little formal power (where there is no parish or town council, local community representatives may apply to begin a neighbourhood forum to prepare a Neighbourhood Plan).

The Secretary of State for Housing, Communities and Local Government oversees the planning system generally, with responsibility for a small number of decisions involving appeals and major infrastructure projects. The Planning Inspectorate for England and Wales (an agency of the Ministry of Housing, Communities and Local Government[16]) decides most appeals on behalf of the Secretary of State. Also at the national level, local governments need to take into account the 2012 National Planning Policy Framework in preparing Local Plans and Neighbourhood Plans. A separate planning framework exists for infrastructure projects of national significance, including major transport infrastructure.

At the local level, the Regional Strategies that imposed requirements on groups of local planning authorities have been removed, although the London Mayor is responsible for creating a strategic plan, and the capital's Local Plans must conform to this.

Local planning authorities outline their intentions through a Local Plan, examined by an independent inspector who assesses whether it meets legal requirements[17] (these may be informed by Neighbourhood Plans (since 2011), which are voted on in local referenda where they comply with local and national policies and legal conditions).

Local authorities can also apply the Community Infrastructure Levy to developments; and Section 106 (of the Town and Country Planning Act 1990) for developers to provide affordable housing or fund services; central government also pays the New Homes Bonus to local authorities to encourage them to build houses.

---

16  Formerly the Department for Communities and Local Government.

17  Especially Part 2 of the Planning and Compulsory Purchase Act 2004 and the Town and Country Planning (Local Planning) (England) Regulations 2012.

Planning applications are not required in all circumstances. When an application is required, the local authority usually makes the decision in the first instance. Applicants may appeal decisions to the Secretary of State through the Planning Inspectorate (where deemed as justifying ministerial attention, appeals can be 'recovered' from the Planning Inspectorate by the Secretary of State).

## References

Airey, J., Scruton, R. and Wales, R. (2018) *Building More, Building Beautiful: How Design and Style Can Unlock the Housing Crisis.* London: Policy Exchange.

Ball, M. (2008) UK planning controls and the market responsiveness of housing supply. Working Papers in Real Estate & Planning 13/08, University of Reading.

Beck, R. and Booth, P. (2019) *Taxation without Justification: An Economic Analysis of the Treasury's Treatment of Privately Rented Housing.* IEA Current Controversies No. 68. London: Institute of Economic Affairs.

Boyfield, K. and Wickham, R. (2019) *Delivering More Homes: Radical Action to Unblock the System.* IEA Current Controversies No. 66. London: Institute of Economic Affairs.

Boys-Smith, N. (2018) What explains the 'design disconnect' between most people and professionals? In *Building Beautiful: A Collection of Essays on the Design, Style and Economics of the Built Environment* (ed. J. Airey). London: Policy Exchange.

Cheshire, P. (2009) Urban containment, housing affordability and price stability – irreconcilable goals. SERC Policy Papers

(SERCPP004). London School of Economics and Political Science, Spatial Economics Research Centre.

Cheshire, P. (2014) Building on Greenbelt land: so where? SERC blog.

Cheshire, P. (2018) Empty homes, longer commutes: one of the many unintended consequences of more restrictive local planning. Presentation by Prof. Paul Cheshire, 28 March. London: Adam Smith Institute.

Davies, S. (2002) Laissez faire urban planning. In *The Voluntary City* (ed. D. T. Beito, P. Gordon and A. Tabarrok). Ann Arbor, MI: University of Michigan Press.

Department for Communities and Local Government (2015) *Plain English Guide to the Planning System*. London: DCLG (https://assets.publishing.service.gov.uk/government/uploads/system/uploads/attachment_data/file/391694/Plain_English_guide_to_the_planning_system.pdf).

Edwards, D. (2017) Brownfield development vs. green belt: what are the pros and cons? *Planning, BIM and Construction Today*, 12 June.

Evans, A. (1988) *No Room! No Room!: The Costs of the British Town and Country Planning System*. London: Institute of Economic Affairs.

Haslehurst, P. (2014) Restoring brownfield sites in our inner towns and cities. *Ideas for Economic Growth*, Issue 10, May. London: Civitas.

Hayek, F. A. (1945) The use of knowledge in society. *American Economic Review* 35(4): 519–30.

Hilber, C. and Vermeulen, W. (2016) The impact of supply constraints on house prices in England. *Economic Journal* 126(591): 358–405.

HMRC (2018) VAT Notice 708: Buildings and Construction. Updated 20 July 2018.

House of Lords Select Committee on Economic Affairs (2016) *Building More Homes*. First Report of Session, 2016–2017.

Jenkins, S. (2004) *Big Bang Localism: A Rescue Plan for British Democracy*. London: Policy Exchange and Localis.

Kynaston, D. (2015) *Modernity Britain 1957–62*. London: Bloomsbury.

McDonagh S. (2018) London's non-green green belt. Siobhan McDonagh MP blog.

Meakin, R. (ed.) (2015) *The Spending Plan*. London: TaxPayers' Alliance.

Meakin, R. (2016) What should a good tax system look like. In *Taxation, Government Spending and Economic Growth* (ed. P. Booth). London: Institute of Economic Affairs.

Myers, J. (2017) *Yes In My Back Yard: How to End the Housing Crisis, Boost the Economy and Win More Votes*. London: London Yimby and Adam Smith Institute.

National Audit Office (2016) Disposal of public land for new homes: a progress report. HC 510, Session 2016–2017, 12 July.

Niemietz, K. (2015) *Reducing Poverty through Policies to Cut the Cost of Living*. Joseph Rowntree Foundation.

Niemietz, K. (2016) *The Housing Crisis: A Briefing*. London: Institute of Economic Affairs.

Papworth, T. (2016) *A Garden of One's Own: Suggestions for Development in the Metropolitan Green Belt*. London: Adam Smith Institute.

Pennington, M. (2002) *Liberating the Land: The Case for Private Land Use Planning*. London: Institute of Economic Affairs.

Terry, F. (2018) Can beautiful homes be built in a factory? In *Building Beautiful: A Collection of Essays on the Design, Style and Economics of the Built Environment* (ed. J. Airey). London: Policy Exchange.

Van Lohuizen, A. (2015) *How Much Help Is Help to Buy? Help to Buy and the Impact on House Prices.* London: Shelter.

Wadsworth, M. (2009) Tax simplification: the case for a land value tax. Adam Smith Institute blog.

PART TWO

THE ESSAYS

## 2 THE LAND PURCHASE ACT[1]

Ben Clements

## Summary

Free-market ideals should not be limited to esoteric debates about what could be achieved in theory. Indeed, competition, decentralisation, accountability and choice can solve the biggest challenges of our time. The cost and inaccessibility of housing are among the greatest challenges of British public policy, yet successive governments have acquiesced to special interests and offered short-term gimmicks instead of radical change.

A free market in housing can democratise homeownership for those who had given up hope. However, despite the need to address deep-seated issues in housing, free-market thinkers also need to create policies that are bold, popular, but politically possible, especially given the wide-ranging free-market movement this could start.

This essay proposes the Land Purchase Act – a market-based policy that centres on how public land can be used to help disadvantaged people acquire housing, and not simply the type of housing that bureaucrats

---

1   Koch Breakthrough Prize Winner.

and central planners think people should live in. Instead, people should be given the opportunity to live in the houses that they want, and that are attractive. That way we can create a new generation of homeowners and fundamentally rewrite the policy-making landscape in housing.

## Introduction

We have a unique advantage of being too disorganised to block the future: an opportunity to rethink, from the ground up, our approach to housing; a paradigm shift that ends the short-term gimmicks and authority of bureaucrats; the chance to offer people a radical, market-based solution to housing and the prospect of homeownership. Free-market approaches to housing are, moreover, the only way to ensure that people acquire the housing they want, rather than bureaucrats deciding what is best for people. We can start a movement that dispels the notion that market-based solutions have no place in housing.

This essay applies free-market principles to address the shortage and unaffordability of housing, and outlines how the government can use the equity it has in land to help people on to the housing ladder. The Land Purchase Act proposed in this essay also outlines how people can live in the homes that they want, meaning that this policy has the power to act as the initial step in restoring social mobility in the UK, encouraging more free-market ideas to follow.

This essay is structured as follows. In the first section, the problems affecting the housing market are outlined – both the problems themselves and how a free market in housing has been thwarted. The next section introduces the policy and how it can achieve two objectives: increasing the amount of land made available and the number of homeowners in the UK. In the final section, the economic benefits of the policy initiative and a free-market vision for housing are elucidated.

The Land Purchase Act policy, this essay will conclude, is the key to a new era of economic progress, providing hope to a new generation of homeowners, in particular those yet to experience the liberating powers of the free market.

## The problem stated

Housing costs in the UK are among the highest in the world, both in absolute terms and relative to average incomes. The UK's population has also grown considerably in recent decades. Between 1990 and 2015, the UK's immigrant population increased from 3.7 million to 8.5 million (Pew Research Center 2016). However, while the country's population has grown and increased the demand for housing, there has not been a commensurate increase in housebuilding in the UK. Inaccessibility to housing is linked to poverty and, more importantly, stands in the way of letting people see their children and grandchildren become property owners. Even those previously resistant to more housebuilding have become aware that the increasing cost of buying a home is detrimental to society. People want to own their own homes and the government should not stand in the way of this natural ambition. In summary, we need to build more and lower the price of housing.

Despite the large backlog of homes that need to be built, the current system of planning permissions and the conceptions of central planners, such as tower blocks, have not delivered the homes that people actually want and that are attractive. Allowing the free market to work will make homes attractive and, crucially, give people choice when it comes to housing.

So, why is it that people cannot acquire the homes that they want? This is because we build what central planners want, which has led to homes that nobody else wants, meaning we miss out on the exciting vision that a free market in housing can offer. This can be explained by how political intervention has obstructed the free market.

## Free markets thwarted

The roots of the UK's housing crisis date back to the 1947 Town and Country Planning Act, which created a framework for the strictest planning laws in the OECD and designated the man in Whitehall as the planner and provider of housing. These laws have significantly reduced the number of homes being built, especially since the 1970s. The Act designated vast swathes of land as green belt, and imposed height controls, constraining incentives to allow development in areas where people wanted to live. As a result, housing does not meet the realities of modern-day economic demand. The strict planning laws explain why house prices have risen so fast in London, where the demand growth is greatest. Yet the disincentives to build remain strong.

There have been a number of attempts by government in recent years to address the shortage and unaffordability of housing, but these have all been steps in the wrong direction. Government solutions, through interventions such as the Help to Buy scheme, changes to inheritance tax and higher taxes on buy-to-let landlords, have made the problems in housing worse, not better. Indeed, most of these initiatives have inflated the demand for housing and created more distortions in the housing market. To cite but one example, the Help to Buy programme increased house prices by more than £8,000, according to Shelter's estimate in 2015 (Van Lohuizen 2015). It is clear that government subsidies in a market with highly inelastic supply will tend to increase the price, while having a negligible impact on quantity.

The average price for homes in the UK has historically been around four times income, although since 2001 the ratio has consistently been above this (Chu 2016). Rising house prices relative to incomes mean that the average household feels a very heavy burden. Houses in the UK are also considerably smaller than those in other European nations. For much of the population, strict planning laws have resulted in overpriced homes, and not the kinds of homes that people want to live in. And they are often located in parts of the country where fewer people want to live. Again, this is the result of government intervention in housing. Instead, a market-based approach that makes more land available, removes government restrictions and allows people to own the homes they want to live in, is the most effective solution to the housing crisis.

The challenge to free-market thinkers, however, is to produce policies that are politically possible. Special interest groups resistant to more home building are well-organised, and proposals to build on green belt land, for example, are already politicised and problematic. We therefore need to demonstrate the power of a market-based approach on a smaller scale before a total revolution in housing is possible. A free-market approach needs, on the one hand, not to replace one short-term gimmick with another; on the other hand, it should propose simple yet popular ideas that politicians cannot resist implementing.

## The Land Purchase Act

The government imposes extensive restrictions that prevent people from getting on the housing ladder, although a number of government departments are some of the largest landowners in the UK. Moreover, large swathes of government-owned land are located in areas where people want to live. This therefore presents an opportunity to use the equity the government has in land to help people onto the housing ladder, especially in areas where there is high demand for housing. This essay proposes the 'Land Purchase Act' – a market-based policy that makes swathes of land available for people to build homes according to their own choice and preferences. This policy has the potential not only to alleviate many of the problems in housing, but also to serve as an example of what market-based policies could achieve for the wider housing market.

There are estimates going back several years that indicate public land could deliver as many as two million new homes, although half a million may be a more reasonable estimate. Such estimates are based on analysis of the public records of the Central Government Estate and the land holdings of the Greater London Authority (GLA), as well as the potential for development of NHS and Local Authority land, although, naturally, not all of this can be released.[2] We assume a somewhat lower figure, but there is no reason for the government to hold all of this land, especially when affordable housing is already beyond the reach of large segments of the population. Releasing surplus or underused public land would considerably improve access to housing.

The value of land in London, and other areas with high demand for housing, is a disproportionate amount of the total value of a property. Thus, although the proposed policy may not be as effective in areas where land is less valuable, it will tend to enable those priced out by the current housing market to live where they actually want to (it is not unreasonable to say that houses should be built in areas where people want to live, and policymakers should not try to fit the workflow of the country around the existing housing stock). With this policy, we can end the gimmicks, build

---

2   Insufficient transparency with relation to the full extent of land and property assets owned by the government remains a drawback in identifying the potential number of sites that could be released to deliver new homes. Data recorded in the central database of government property and land do not include all public land holdings.

houses in the right places, and, crucially, allow people to live in the types of homes they actually prefer.

## How it works

The government will enter into a contract with the occupier, who will take out a mortgage to cover the cost of building the property on the land. Under the policy, the occupier will build the home they wish to live in, rather than the bureaucratic imposition of having the government decide what is built. The occupier will be given a choice over the timescale and structure of how they gradually acquire ownership of the land. The composition of this process provides the occupier with options: they could pay some rent for the land, choose to purchase the land at set intervals over time, or buy the land at a discounted rate if they have lived there for a set period of time, for instance twenty or thirty years. This policy applies market principles to the government's equity in land to help people flexibly acquire housing, especially in difficult areas.

The Land Purchase Act would also reduce the number of planning restrictions on houses built on land made available under the policy. Currently, hundreds of pages of planning legislation exist for each local authority, in keeping with the command-and-control economics of the original 1947 Town and Country Planning Act. Planning permissions enforce exceedingly specific details about the development or expansion of properties. Removing such planning permissions from homes built under the Land

Purchase Act would, however, ensure that such homes respond to market demands instead of what the council or a bureaucrat thinks individuals need. Inefficiencies in building homes would be removed and modernisation allowed in UK land development.

This policy offers people a hand-up instead of a handout, and puts them on a path to homeownership, not government dependency.

## Economic benefits

Making more land available to be built on would unleash a series of economic benefits to boost the wider economy and help the disadvantaged in society. Given that the policy would be more effective in areas around major cities, it would also help boost productivity. Productivity is notably higher in cities than rural areas (some estimates put the average labour productivity of urban areas at five percentage points higher than rural areas) (ONS 2017: 2). Higher productivity in major cities also translates into increased investment and the potential for greater economic specialisation. This productivity growth would not be limited to the boundaries of the city and would spill over to boost the economies of surrounding areas. Thus both major cities and their surrounding areas would benefit from higher economic growth as their potential for expansion is increased.

More people would be able to become homeowners as a result of the policy, which would considerably improve the household financial stability of the new occupiers. Making more land available at a discounted rate and lowering the cost of housebuilding by removing planning requirements is the key to achieving this. The lower cost of housebuilding would make it easier for a new occupier to be approved for mortgages. This would free up the incomes of those spending a high proportion of their wages on rent to instead acquire a home, still the largest asset for most households. Furthermore, making housing affordable in areas where land is particularly expensive increases the mobility of the population. Lowering the cost of acquiring a home under this policy would also free up the incomes of new occupiers for other activities, for instance increasing consumption for a better quality of life, or giving them the capital to start a business. By making more land available, economic dynamism is unleashed at the lower end of the income spectrum, improving financial stability and welfare.

The wider availability of housing targeted at those currently receiving some form of government assistance would also help alleviate the pressure on the existing social housing stock. Although a free-market approach to housing could increase the proportion of the population becoming homeowners, creating a pathway to homeownership for people receiving government assistance would make social housing more readily available to the most vulnerable in society. In addition, the wider availability of land to be built on would increase construction.

## Towards free-market housing

For those who believe in free markets, it is, however, an anomaly that much housing is firmly under state control and provision. The primary reason land is so expensive is because the government has constrained its supply by bureaucratic fiat. A free market in housing is the remedy to the current government-imposed command-and-control approach. Removing government restrictions and liberating the market would increase the supply of land, lower the price of acquiring a home, and allow people to build homes they want, which are aesthetically pleasing.

It is clear that releasing surplus or underused public land, through the mechanisms outlined above, would alleviate the inaccessibility and cost of housing. This is the right policy for politicians who are only now catching up with voters in recognising the need to build more homes. Although the idea of more housebuilding used to be vigorously opposed in the Home Counties, for example, people now wonder why it is not already happening. Becoming a homeowner remains one of the most important routes to greater social mobility and increased prosperity.

The policy proposed in this essay gives politicians a solution. The proposal does not require a political revolution. Free-market proponents need to focus on what is achievable and generate a critical mass of people ready for free-market change. Then we can tackle the green belt, zoning laws and permissions, to create a truly free market in housing. Let the planners and providers in Whitehall defend their record in housing. They will be left to catch up with their electorates as housing policy moves on to its free-market future.

# References

Chu, B. (2016) The one chart that shows how UK houses are now even more unaffordable. *The Independent*, 28 April.

Office for National Statistics (2017) *Exploring Labour Productivity in Rural and Urban Areas in Great Britain: 2014*. Fareham: ONS.

Pew Research Center (2016) 5 facts about migration and the United Kingdom (https://www.pewresearch.org/fact-tank/2016/06/21/5-facts-about-migration-and-the-united-king dom/).

Van Lohuizen, A. (2015) *How Much Help Is Help to Buy? Help to Buy and the Impact on House Prices*. London: Shelter.

# 3 PRESUMED PERMISSION: A SELF-BUILD FRAMEWORK FOR LOCAL DEVELOPMENT RIGHTS[1]

Stephen Ashmead

## Summary

Although the UK is in the grip of a housing crisis, too few homes are being built by too few developers. We build fewer homes per capita than comparable countries, and our homes are smaller and of poorer quality.

The planning process works on the presumption that new homes cannot be built unless home builders go through a maze of bureaucracy. It pits individuals who want to build their own homes in their own communities against large-scale developers with the resources to game the system. This leads to monolithic and soulless estates instead of thoughtfully designed homes in organically growing communities. As a result, we have one of the lowest self-build rates in Europe.

A framework of permitted new builds, as an extension to permitted development rights, would allow self-builders to fast-track their planning applications. The presumption

---

1    Highly Commended Prize Winner.

would be that people *can* build their own homes unless these are demonstrably inappropriate for their community.

The framework would be incorporated into local plans, allowing homes to be built in vernacular styles and blend into the local environment, increasing local powers over development and overcoming Nimbyism.

## Introduction

The UK's housing crisis is a product of its uniquely dysfunctional housing system. While our neighbours build good quality homes for their citizens, the UK fails. We build half the homes we need and the few homes we eke out are often of poor quality. One of the particular anomalies of our housing system is the chronically low rate of self-builds. In Austria, 80 per cent of new homes are self-built, in France 60 per cent. Even in densely populated cities such as Berlin, individuals and groups are routinely able to build their own homes (Wilson 2017). Yet the UK, in the grip of a housing crisis, only achieves 7–10 per cent self-build homes (ibid.). There is no lack of desire for self-built homes; a recent poll suggested that if the number of self-builds increased, support for new builds would also grow (Ipsos MORI 2016). Nor is there a lack of support for new homes, if they are well-designed and appropriate for their environment (Airey et al. 2018).

The UK could be a nation of proud housebuilders and homeowners. This essay suggests that this could be achieved without a single sentence passing through parliament, if local planning authorities and communities join together to allow individuals to self-build their own homes. None of the ideas in this essay are therefore new, except perhaps in how different elements of our existing system can be used together to maximise housebuilding. This essay proposes a framework for presumed permission for self-builds, a model which involves:

- The creation of 'form-based' self-build frameworks, outlining permitted small-scale developments.
- Self-build designs or modifications to existing dwellings which meet the local framework receiving a light-touch 'notification' process for planning consent.
- Presumed consent for self-build designs which meet the local development rights, regardless of current land use, excepting common sense restrictions, and thus moving away from land-based permission.
- Local planning authorities promoting the local development rights both at the design stage and through supporting self-builders.

There are many advantages to these presumed permission self-build frameworks. Firstly, they allow individuals to build or adapt their own homes in their own communities. Self-builds allow individuals to bypass large-scale developers or the need for state intervention, creating a flexible, direct route to home building and homeownership. The local development rights would create certainty for self-builders, who would know from the outset whether their proposed new home met the criteria in their neighbourhood. If self-build rates rose to meet those across Europe, the UK would double its housing output.

Secondly, this is politically feasible. The powers to bring presumed permission into fruition already exist. This proposal assumes that legislation would only be required to compel local planning authorities to use them. Communities would have democratic grassroots control over new builds upstream in the planning system, by establishing what housing is needed for their community, reducing Nimbyism and providing certainty over new design. Form-based frameworks allow communities to shape the look and feel of new builds in a coherent way that people can understand and support. Promoting self-build would be politically popular and reduce concerns around inappropriate, large-scale developments. People building their own homes are more invested in the quality of their home, are making a commitment to the community they will live in, and know best what will meet their needs.

Thirdly, allowing people the opportunity to self-build would reinvigorate the housing market generally. The restrictiveness of the planning system means that land awarded planning permission is approximately one hundred times more valuable than land without (Onward 2018). Creating a system of presumed permission for self-builds would reduce the scarcity of land supply and thus reduce land prices. Large developers, whose current unique selling point is their ability to purchase land, would be competing against a newly powerful self-build industry, leading to better quality homes and innovative design. Once there is a steady supply of self-build homes, large housebuilders could be less inclined to slow the release of new homes onto the market as the 'absorption rate' of the local market would be less affected by the appearance of new homes (Letwin 2018).

But perhaps the biggest impact of presumed permission for self-builds would be its effect on the national psyche. We are currently a nation which seems unable to build the homes it needs, while other countries manage to do so perfectly well. A pernicious fatalism has set in, undermining the country's ability to find a solution. A strong policy promoting self-build would signal that building and owning one's home is a right; that individuals should aspire to creating their own homes; and that, with a can-do attitude, we can solve the housing crisis in our own communities without outside intervention.

## Why do we have a housing crisis?

The UK's highly restrictive planning system was introduced as a reaction to fears that ugly urban sprawl was eating into the countryside (Ellis n.d.), and it was in part designed to make self-building hard (Toms 2018). The system requires that every change to the built environment is scrutinised and open to challenge. The impact on the housing market is thus essentially twofold. Firstly, only large-scale developers can overcome the burdens imposed by the current system and the lack of certainty it creates (initially, this was mitigated by large-scale housebuilding by the state, but this has ultimately turned out to be a temporary fix). Secondly, it creates a limited supply of land on which building is allowed, inflating land prices, which again favours the large developers able to afford such excessive values.

Accordingly, the UK builds only half the new homes needed. Those that are built are frequently built to a poor standard as developers try to squeeze as many homes as possible onto overvalued land. This has led to widespread concerns about housebuilding among locals, whose only say in the planning process is downstream through objecting to new proposals.[2] Nimbyism has therefore become an entrenched feature of the planning system despite widespread support for new homes. The current restrictive, top-down planning system has failed. Creating a new, bottom-up system would reinvigorate house building and homeownership.

## Reinvigorating self-build through community-designed Local Development Rights

National permitted development rights already exist, although limited in scope and, in the case of converting offices to residential dwellings, time.[3] However, since 1990, local planning authorities have had the power to introduce Local Development Orders (LDOs) to grant additional permitted development rights. Despite the flexibility and extensive powers LDOs offer, and despite being promoted through the localism agenda, uptake has been low. LDOs tend to be used for niche development purposes

2    Somewhat ironically, if you want to build a dwelling for cows instead of humans, your permitted development rights are much more extensive and straightforward.

3    Town and Country Planning Act 1990 section 61A (https://www.legislation .gov.uk/ukpga/1990/8/part/III/crossheading/local-development-orders).

and, apart from a few LDOs such as Graven Hill in Oxfordshire (Graven Hill n.d.), have thus far offered little for self-builders. The Localism Act 2011 further introduced Neighbourhood Development Orders and Community Right to Build Orders. Again, uptake has been poor in the face of substantial bureaucracy. For example, proposed Community Right to Build Orders in rural areas still need to be granted 'exception site' status (HACT 2013).

Instead of focusing on the status of the land on which a new-build would be developed, presumed permission self-build frameworks would focus on establishing appropriate designs for small developments. A self-build framework, similar to the powers listed above, would set out what a community considers appropriate, with only minimal common-sense restrictions on where the new homes may be built.[4]

Under this proposal, communities would have direct control over designing a permitted development framework for self-builds for their community, upstream in the planning process.[5] The current Nimbyism in our planning system stems from the lack of community input early on in this planning process. People have little say on changes in their community until far too late, and then only through contesting proposals that have been made, creating

---

4 The restrictions on where current permitted development rights can be applied, such as national parks, flood plains or to listed buildings, would be a useful starting point.

5 Local planning authorities already have an obligation to consult when proposing an LDO; however, for these new self-build frameworks, consultation is integral to the design and acceptability of the proposal.

uncertainty and fear over future developments. Unfortunately, the poor quality of new-builds in our country today does little to assuage locals' concerns. Yet recent research shows that people support new builds if they are aesthetically pleasing and fit in with their surroundings. Furthermore, there is consensus around what types of homes are suitable in different community settings (Airey et al. 2018). Through engaging with local communities, a broad, popular code can be developed that meets communities' needs for new housing but also their desire to preserve their existing heritage.

The self-build framework would be 'form-based', setting out the physical form of new buildings. Form-based codes in particular help to achieve community approval because they are intuitive and because they focus on how new-builds integrate with their surroundings. For example, standards in rural communities would probably emphasise local vernacular styles or traditional building methods, while urban sites for regeneration may instead encourage innovative construction methods or sustainable design. As the framework would be form-based, it would be sufficiently flexible to cover a range of designs and circumstances. These frameworks should also cover any home improvements or changes of use up to a new build, such as conversions, extensions and use changes, from building a granny annexe in the garden to a barn conversion.

As mentioned, creating local development rights specifically for self-builders would be politically popular. The idea of self-build is itself popular, with 52 per cent of people saying they would consider building their own home (Wilson 2017). This popularity would also inspire local communities to develop frameworks: those who would most benefit from self-build frameworks would be people already living in, having connections to, or being attracted to an area, because of the type of community it offers. In turn, this would provide stronger assurances that the homes built through this framework would be appropriate to the community and genuinely address the housing need of people who live there or want to live there. Through the form-based self-build frameworks, communities would be reassured that new-builds would neither be ugly, poor quality boxes, nor Grand Designs–inspired vanity projects. Self-build homes would be built incrementally, instead of as a single, large and disruptive development, allowing communities to naturally absorb new housing. And self-build homes could be more creative in their use of land, for example through using odd plots of vacant or underutilised land which would be unprofitable for a large-scale developer.

The benefits of self-build frameworks for the self-builders themselves would be even more apparent. Once designed, these self-build frameworks would create new, locally designed, permitted development rights. These rights would create a way for self-builders to bypass the normal planning route – they would simply have to notify the local planning authority of their intention to build according to the framework and pay a small fee to cover administration costs. The self-build framework would dramatically reduce bureaucracy for aspiring home builders, and provide certainty that their plans would gain consent. This certainty would feed into other aspects of the self-build project, including timescales, costs and access to finance.

## A new role for the local planner

Self-build frameworks would release local planning authorities from the bureaucratic task of scrutinising planning applications for small developments. Local authorities should be encouraged to promote the frameworks (creating a new statutory duty if necessary), both through supporting communities to design them and through helping self-builders find land and develop their plans to meet the local self-build framework.

Additionally, self-build frameworks would help to draw together the increased local powers granted by government over the last ten years into a single coherent policy. Building on the 'Right to Build' established in the Housing and Planning Act 2016, where local authorities are required to meet the demand of individuals and associations seeking to acquire land for self- and custom-builds, permitted development frameworks would allow local authorities actively to assist aspiring self-builders to find land and design their new home in accordance with the frameworks in their communities. Again, self-build frameworks coupled with the General Power of Competence set out in the 2011 Localism Act would further empower local government to support people living in their own communities to build their own homes.[6]

---

6  This could, for example, include setting up a local-authority-owned company for acquiring and selling plots to self-builders, or providing loans to self-builders or associations of self-builders.

## The wider-reaching benefits of a presumed permission self-build framework

The benefits of presumed permission for self-builders are self-evident. Self-builders would have a near-certain route to planning permission as long as their plans meet the requirements of their local self-build framework. Such liberalisation of the planning process would lead to an increase in both housing supply and homeownership, as people are able to build their own homes for themselves. The UK has an unusually low level of self-build construction, so it is unlikely that even large increases in the supply of self-build homes would lead to a drop in new homes constructed by other developers, and indeed, as discussed below, may increase supply from other sources.

Local communities would have greater democratic control over future development in their neighbourhoods and be able to develop a distinctive future identity. The self-build framework would promote better land use, particularly in areas with high land values, including replacing poor quality homes, adding storeys to existing homes, or building on small brownfield plots. This would maximise the potential of already developed land, further reducing the need for future sprawl or inappropriate development. Communities would be given a route to promote innovative design through the local self-build framework, such as eco-homes or offsite construction methods.

Self-build frameworks would also reduce land prices. Land with planning permission attracts such a premium because of its scarcity. As nearly all land would have presumed permission for self-build developments, land prices would adjust to take this into account. If local authorities decided to buy land to release to self-builders, they could be able to do so at closer to existing use values, as the land's value might not increase so markedly if sold on as individual plots.[7] With greater certainty surrounding self-builds, it should also become easier for self-builders to acquire finance to fund the construction of their new home. This would create a virtuous circle: as self-build construction became a more established route, mortgage and loan products for self-builds would become more mainstream.

Although the framework is specifically intended to help boost the number of self-build homeowners, the framework could also benefit larger developers. UK developers are less likely to use innovative building techniques than elsewhere (Pan et al. 2007), and, as previously noted, they build homes of a lower quality. A system that provides presumed permission for self-builds would also reinvigorate large-scale developers as the housebuilding market is opened up to a wider range of consumers: the additional competition from self-builders would promote innovation, as the unique selling point of large housebuilders would no longer be their ability to acquire plots of land. The framework would act as a signal for local appetite for development in both scale and style, allowing developers and planning authorities to prioritise developments that meet local

---

7    While not within the scope of this proposal, there are logical extensions to this policy which could include large developers providing serviced plots for self-builders as Section 106 contributions, or encouraging housing associations or community land trusts to buy land on behalf of self-builders.

needs, making the planning process more straightforward, and leading to large-scale developments which are more customised to their community.

But, to reiterate, perhaps the biggest impact of presumed permission for small developments would be its effect on the national psyche. We currently believe we are unable to solve our housing crisis, while other countries seem perfectly capable of building quality homes (Letwin 2018). Elsewhere, even in densely populated cities, individuals and groups are routinely able to build their own homes. Self-build frameworks would provide a democratic route for communities to shape the future identity of their neighbourhoods, and home building and homeownership would be increased. Having a clear policy advocating self-build would send a strong signal that individuals can aspire to create their own homes, and build a new can-do attitude to home building and homeownership.

## References

Airey, J., Scruton, R. and Wales, R. (2018) *Building More, Building Beautiful*. London: Policy Exchange (https://policyexchange .org.uk/wp-content/uploads/2018/09/Building-More-Build ing-Beautiful-for-print.pdf).

Ellis, H. (n.d.) *The Rise and Fall of the 1947 Planning System*. London: Historic England (https://historicengland.org.uk/whats -new/debate/recent/town-and-country-planning-act -70th-anniversary/rise-and-fall-of-1947-planning-system).

Graven Hill (n.d.) About Graven Hill (https://www.gravenhill. co.uk/about-graven-hill/).

HACT (2013) *Community Right to Build Case Studies.* London: HACT (https://www.hact.org.uk/community-right-build-ca se-studies).

Ipsos MORI (2016) *Survey of Self-Build Intentions 2016.* London: Ipsos MORI (https://www.ipsos.com/ipsos-mori/en-uk/sur vey-self-build-intentions-2016).

Letwin, O. (2018) *Independent Review of Build Out Rates: Draft Analysis.* London: Ministry of Housing, Communities and Local Government (https://assets.publishing.service.gov.uk/ government/uploads/system/uploads/attachment_data/ file/718878/Build_Out_Review_Draft_Analysis.pdf).

Onward (2018) Sharing land value with communities: an open letter, 12 January. London: Onward (http://www.ukonward .com/landreform/).

Pan, W., Gibb, A. G. F. and Dainty, A. R. J. (2007) Perspectives of UK housebuilders on the use of offsite modern methods of construction. *Construction Management and Economics* 25(2): 183–94.

Toms, K. (2018) If Britain wants more self-build housing, we need to change its planning system. *CityMetric*, 16 March (https:// www.citymetric.com/fabric/if-britain-wants-more-self-bu ild-housing-we-need-change-its-planning-system-3767).

Wilson, W. (2017) Self-build and custom build housing (England), House of Commons Library Briefing Paper 06784 (http:// researchbriefings.files.parliament.uk/documents/SN06784/ SN06784.pdf).

# 4 SIMPLIFIED PLANNING ZONES AND THE REALIGNMENT OF FISCAL INCENTIVES[1]

Daniel Pycock and Charles Shaw

## Summary

This essay analyses the UK housing market, examines current housing policies, and suggests politically feasible reforms that would increase the proportion of homeowners and number of houses built in the UK.

The UK is in the midst of an acute housing affordability crisis which is particularly evident in London and southeast England. The main causes of this crisis are policies implemented over several decades to contain urban expansion.

We demonstrate that the UK's land-use policies and fiscal incentives distort the housing market, while the planning system adversely affects house building and homeownership.

The government has introduced policies to address these issues, but the majority are costly, ineffective and welfare-reducing, if not outright amplifiers of the original problems.

---

1 Highly Commended Prize Winner.

This essay argues that the UK should introduce a system of Simplified Planning Zones which would eliminate the need for land-use planning permission, and exclude Section 106 and other complications from planning permission for development.

Beyond these Simplified Planning Zones, the essay also argues for the realignment of fiscal incentives at local level to encourage local authorities to approve applications in the development control framework that prevails.

## The current state of the housing market

The UK is notable for its complex planning regime focused on urban containment. This uses the development control framework established by the Town and Country Planning Act, enforced by local authorities using development plans, 'green belt' designations,[2] height and density restrictions, and protected views schemes. Against this backdrop, a key long-term political concern is the lack of affordable dwellings for purchase or rent. UK house prices are extraordinarily high, and housing in London and the southeast of England is some of the most expensive and cramped in the world.

Internationally, a 'comparable apartment' in London trails only Hong Kong and Monaco in price, and Hong

---

2  The first green belts were established around London, Birmingham and Sheffield in the 1930s. The Green Belt (London and Home Counties) Act and the Town and Country Planning Act then allowed local authorities to purchase land and include land in development plans for green belt purposes. In 1955, government circular 42/55 asked local authorities to consider protecting land by the 'formal designation of clearly-defined green belts'.

Kong and Bermuda in rents (Global Property Index 2017). Housing costs are also high when measured relative to income. A standard measure of affordability is the ratio of median house price to median annual full-time earnings. In fifteen years, that ratio has increased from 5.06 to 7.78 in England and Wales, and 6.38 to 10.26 in southeast England. In London, where affordability is at its worst since records began, the ratio has grown from 6.57 to 12.36, while the median rent-to-income ratio has climbed from 1:5 to 1:3 (ONS 2018).

The current lack of housing affordability has not developed overnight. UK house prices have grown faster than in any other OECD country over the last four decades, and have strongly outperformed real GDP per capita growth.[3] However, UK house prices are also extremely volatile. As Hilber and Vermeulen (2016) have demonstrated, volatility in real UK house prices is significantly higher than the most volatile areas of the US. The cause of this is the decline in per capita terms of housebuilding since the 1970s, as well as the concomitant 'lack of supply responsiveness to changes in demand' identified by Barker (2004).

On average, people in employment could expect to pay approximately 7.6 times earnings to buy a home in England and Wales in 2016, up from 3.6 times in 1997. The median price for residential property in England and Wales increased by 259 per cent between 1997 and 2016; median earnings increased by 68 per cent in the same period.

---

3   In the period 1967 to 1982, UK house prices grew at an average annual rate of 7.88 per cent. In the period 1982 to 2017, they grew at an average annual rate of 8.91 per cent.

During the period 1967 to 1991, the UK built approximately 5.7 million new-build dwellings. The population increased by 4.5 per cent, or 2.5 million people, in this period. From 1991 to 2016, the UK built just over 3.5 million dwellings, with population growth of 14.3 per cent, or 8.2 million people (Cheshire et al. 2018). Taking into account factors such as densification, this implies a shortfall of at least three million housing units before considering the ongoing deficit between housing starts and population growth.[4] The average market participant, then, lives in artificially cramped housing and is priced out from upsizing.[5] In the meantime, the young and highly skilled are displaced into suboptimal living arrangements by ever-increasing rents (MCHLG 2018).

This is an important point, not least because, since 2011, spatial misallocation has limited the number working in London's scientific, technological, engineering, research and other sectors. This hurts productivity and is estimated

---

4    The impact of immigration is beyond the scope of this paper. The microeconomic evidence is that house prices are subject to a negative income effect (Sa 2011). There is also a narrative for London between 1951 and 2011 with net population growth ≈ 0.0 per cent and a real rise in house prices of 463 per cent (Cheshire et al. 2018). The macroeconomic case is inconclusive, but would indicate that immigration does push up average house prices.

5    The problem is aggravated by the deadweight loss of the highly inefficient Stamp Duty Land Tax, which adversely affects short distance moves and impedes other housing transactions. It is worth noting that UK revenue from SDLT has tripled in recent years from £2.9 billion (2008/09) to £8.6 billion (2016/17). But, to quantify the loss in economic terms, Hilber and Lyytikäinen (2017) found that with assumptions regarding the value of forgone transactions, the welfare loss was roughly 80 per cent of the revenue raised. Best and Kleven (2017) also find sizeable welfare losses, although they do not report numbers that would allow us to access the marginal cost of public funds. See also Mirrlees et al. (2011) and Besley et al. (2014).

to have reduced aggregate UK GDP by between 13 per cent and 30 per cent (Hsieh and Moretti 2018; Myers 2017). On the margins of market clearing, meanwhile, are those who approach, but never quite reach, the deposit requirements to purchase their first home.

But what has caused the decline in house building that we have identified? From a production perspective, the factor of land has increased in price from the equivalent of 50 per cent to 200 per cent of GDP in the last fifty years (Cheshire 2009; Schumacher 2018). To dig deeper, however, we need to look at the planning system.

## How the planning system works

The first stage of the planning system arises from land use regulations of the Town and Country Planning (Use Classes) Order, which prescribes and designates categories for land use. If an individual plans to convert commercial premises or farmland to housing, they first require permission related to land use. The building plans are then submitted to the local planning authority (LPA), which 'assesses the plan to ensure it is in keeping with development plans, existing infrastructure, permitted use, dimensions and materials as appropriate to the area', and reaches a decision (MCHLG 2012). If the decision is objected to, it can be appealed, firstly to the Planning Inspectorate, and ultimately to the Secretary of State for Housing, Communities and Local Government.

There are many problems with how this system works in practice. In economic terms, we know that the restriction of land supply is a key factor. There is an unavoidable aspect to this, including the prohibitive cost of developing brownfield sites and the unfeasibility of building on certain topographies.[6] Yet there is also an aspect that is unnecessary and artificial. A study of the distribution of green belt designation, for instance, would show that the inclination of an LPA to protect undeveloped land with green belt designation is positively correlated with the acuteness of local housing need.[7] Assuming the obstacle of land use has been overcome in the design stage, however, there are then hurdles to acquiring planning permission for the development itself.

One hurdle could include, for instance, the objections of local residents. Another could be Section 106 obligations (see Chapter 1). The largest hurdle, however, is the uncertainty of the outcome of the planning committee(s) of the LPA(s) themselves. The evidence shows that the proportion of planning applications rejected by LPAs is, again, positively correlated to the acuteness of housing need (Cheshire et al. 2018). Moreover, Hilber and Vermeulen (2016) have estimated that regulatory constraints were responsible for over half the increase in UK house prices from 1974 to 2008. This suggests not only that UK house prices would be 35 per cent lower had the planning system been abolished, but

---

6   For example, about 17 per cent of land is peat bog, moor and heathland; 13 per cent is woodland and forests; another percentage is unsuitable due to gradient or elevation (etc.).

7   The average amount of green belt that is arable land (i.e. suitable for development) is 35 per cent. It is higher in, for example, Cambridge (74 per cent) and Oxford (44 per cent).

also that house prices in the southeast of England would be 25 per cent lower if it had the regulatory restrictiveness (or lack thereof) of the northeast.

But what is behind this regional problem? A lack of incentives, for one. There are weak incentives for local authorities to approve residential development. Under the current arrangements, local authorities are funded by fees, local taxes and central government grants – the formulae of which offset any medium-term gains from expanding the council tax base. Moreover, the cost of infrastructure for residential developments may be borne by local authorities, which means that developments become a net loss. This empowers the Nimby representations made by local residents (often acting rationally by protecting the value of their housing investment), with which planning officers are often inclined to concur. All these factors mean that the planning system is arguably responsible for 70 per cent of the increase in UK house prices since the 1970s. The planning system is thus the foremost factor.

## Other problems with the housing market

There are multiple problems with the housing market, notwithstanding the negative effects of the planning system. Perhaps the most obvious is a lack of political leadership, represented by the fact that Kit Malthouse, Minister of State for Housing from July 2018 to July 2019, was the seventeenth occupant of that office in two decades. Then there are further aspects of the planning system that place an obligation on residential developers to allocate a percentage to 'affordable housing'. This is negotiated with the local planning authority. The outcome is uncertain and unknown until very late in the process, so developers can only estimate land prices and secure working capital for the project at the last minute.

**Figure 9    Annual dividends for the top five housebuilders as a share of profits**

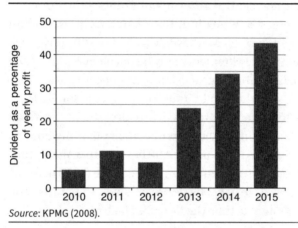

*Source*: KPMG (2008).

This is particularly onerous for small housebuilding firms, and constitutes a significant barrier to entry. It partly explains the trend of high-volume builders growing from a 31 per cent market share in 2008 to over 60 per cent today, and it is why the House of Lords (2016) concluded that the market had 'all the characteristics of an oligopoly' (see Figure 9). In such circumstances, the Lords continued, 'it is rational for private enterprise to optimise profits rather than volume, [and to limit] their uncertainty in a market characterised by constant Government intervention and cyclical risk'. The future, if industry consolidation is not tackled, is one of contrived scarcity to maximise profitability per unit over volume, and competitors lacking access to finance and land. Yet this is not all.

As recession faded, an increasing proportion of profits was distributed to investors, rather than reinvested to boost output. Using KPMG's costs (2008) and Barratt's (2015) average housebuilding cost per unit of £52,000, we can estimate development costs per unit to be £104,000. Applying the average cost to the biggest housebuilders, the £936 million distributed to shareholders in 2015 could have funded an additional 9,000 dwellings (6 per cent of output).

Meanwhile, from 2013 to Q2 2017 inclusive, 135,000 homes were sold under Help to Buy. The four biggest housebuilders over the same period saw their combined pre-tax profits increase by 388 per cent. In 2016, 56 per cent of Persimmon homes and 44 per cent of Barratt homes were sold under Help to Buy (and over 25 per cent of Help to Buy homes have been sold as leaseholds).

Government policies intended to alleviate the housing affordability crisis have often made it worse. Help to Buy was introduced in 2013 to improve the balance sheet of borrowers and to stimulate housing demand. The scheme consisted of multiple options, the most generous of which allowed aspiring owners to purchase a new-build home with a 5 per cent deposit. Housing subsidies such as these have perverse effects. When housing markets are tightly regulated and where there is inflexible supply, subsidies have the effect of reducing homeownership (Hilber and

Turner 2014).[8] The government has long argued for such schemes due to their potential ability to reduce the risk of household income exposure to house prices. Yet Benetton et al. (2018) show that these were predominantly used by households to buy properties they would otherwise not have been able to afford. Hence, contrary to its stated objectives, Help to Buy has improved neither borrowers' balance sheets nor household risk exposure.[9]

## Suggested policy response

The UK requires housebuilding on a scale analogous to the 1950s, when then Minister for Housing and Local Government Harold MacMillan was tasked with building 300,000 homes per annum. It requires the volume of construction achieved by the New Town Corporations of the 1960s, executed with the market nous of the London Docklands Development Corporation in the 1980s. The current target for new dwellings of 300,000 per annum is inadequate, and should be increased to 500,000 to account for historical undersupply. Development ought to be driven by private sector financing under a demand-led planning regime.

Yet such suggestions in themselves are not policies. Moreover, it is important to highlight the fact that if there

---

8   Furthermore, in markets with less regulation and flexible supply, subsidies have a positive effect on homeownership only for the highest income quantile groups, thus making the policy regressive regardless.

9   Regrettably, there are multiple issues (among them Stamp Duty Land Tax, the importance of technology, etc.) that, for the sake of brevity, we must overlook.

were a 'silver bullet' policy which would increase home-ownership and be politically feasible, such a policy would have been included in a manifesto. There can therefore only be multiple policies to improve the number of houses built and the rate of homeownership.[10] This essay therefore recommends a three-pronged policy response to alleviate the housing shortage and rejuvenate our property-owning democracy. When analysed alone, these recommendations would be necessary but not sufficient. If implemented in a mutually reinforcing way, however, they would lead to a material process of conversion and change.

The first recommendation is a simplification of the planning process. This can be achieved effectively by eliminating 'development control' and instituting a rules-based and market-oriented zoning system. The implementation of this would be feasible through Simplified Planning Zone (SPZ) pilot schemes in certain local authorities, to be followed by a roll-out across the country. It would ensure the efficient allocation of land and a simplified planning process with higher certainty of outcome. It would also alleviate the artificial scarcity of land and remove the need to acquire planning permission for any change of land use.

Instead, certain areas would be marked for residential use, and – within those zones – there would be an automatic presumption of development. The objections

---

10  It is also important to draw attention at this point to false solutions. The idea that brownfield sites could – even at 100 per cent utilisation – provide 60 per cent of estimated housing need or that expropriating 200,000 privately owned, unoccupied homes, would remotely make a significant impact on the housing crisis is not correct.

of neighbours could only proceed if the developer is in articulable breach of building regulations. This would remove the need for lengthy public consultations and also eliminate negotiations for Section 106, thereby alleviating delays that hit the largest developments and smallest housebuilding firms hardest, and invigorating supply-side market competitiveness.

The second recommendation, which is conditional on the pilot scheme phase of the first, is that central government obliges local authorities to critically review their designated green belts, height and density restrictions, 'protected view' corridors, and other planning constraints, for market failure.[11] This can be implemented either by government circular or through inclusion in the National Planning Policy Framework. Where areas of market failure are identified, and development could reasonably be argued to exceed opportunity costs, the government should then consider imposing an SPZ. This should especially be the case in London, where a relaxation of the Metropolitan Green Belt on just 5 per cent of its land would be enough to provide over 1 million new homes at unambitious densities within 15 minutes' walk of an existing tube or railway station (Papworth 2016).

The third and final recommendation is to reintroduce fiscal incentives at local level to permit development. This would stimulate housebuilding outside SPZs by aligning local tax revenues per capita to residential development.

---

11 A lack of buy-in from local authorities could necessitate a nationwide survey for planning failure either by the Planning Inspectorate or an independent body.

It would incentivise LPAs not only to approve more good planning applications, but also to encourage them and improve them, even under a development control framework. In nearly all cases, there are no such incentives in place in the UK. The only local tax is based on (outdated) property values and, compared internationally, this is irrelevant to the UK tax framework. As such, the Mirrlees Review (Mirrlees et al. 2011) recommended it ought to have more weight, and this essay endorses these proposals.

This essay further advises that such proposals could be implemented in a revenue-neutral way either by adjusting the formulae with which central government grants are awarded, by introducing a residential development precept on new builds, or by the introduction of a value added tax on housing consumption. This would give councils full control over their council tax revenues and prevent central government from offsetting extra revenue in the medium term against the funding given to councils by grant. This scheme should be run alongside the initiative proposed by Bosetti and Sims (2016) to train councillors and officers such that they have the expertise to confidently guide developers towards high quality development.

The reform of the housing market also needs to include the elimination of demand side (e.g. Help to Buy) and supply side (e.g. Starter Homes Land Fund) subsidies. It needs to see a reinvigoration of competitiveness on the supply side and the removal of unhelpful barriers and regulations that get in the way of building homes. It might be more efficient, for instance, to see a fairly uniform densification of existing urban areas, the transformation of brownfield sites into urban green space and for construction to take place on a small percentage of the green belt. The core argument of this essay, however, is that we can and have to find a feasible and Pareto-improving way of reforming the planning system. This is because housing is highly income elastic (OBR 2014), and therefore the improvement of affordability is almost entirely dependent on supply. With incentives and training for local authorities to encourage development on the one hand, and SPZs on the other, we believe we have struck the right balance to enable housebuilders to build, for house prices to gradually adjust in a more competitive market, for housing affordability to improve relative to income, and therefore for homeownership to increase.

## References

Barker, K. (2004) *Review of Housing Supply: Delivering Stability: Securing Our Future Housing Needs*. London: HMSO (http://news.bbc.co.uk/nol/shared/bsp/hi/pdfs/17_03_04_barker_review.pdf).

Benetton, M., Bracke, P., Cocco, J. and Garbarino, N. (2018) Housing affordability and shared equity mortgages. Paper presented at the NIESR/RICS/CaCHE/CFM 'Broken' Housing Market Conference 2018, London, June.

Besley, T., Meads, N. and Surico, P. (2014) The incidence of transaction taxes: evidence from a Stamp Duty holiday. *Journal of Public Economics* 119: 61–70 (http://eprints.lse.ac.uk/59637/1/Besley_Incidence%20transaction_2016.pdf).

Best, M. C. and Kleven, H. K. (2017) Housing market responses to transaction taxes: evidence from notches and stimulus in the

UK. *Review of Economic Studies* 85(1): 157–93 (https://www
.henrikkleven.com/uploads/3/7/3/1/37310663/best-kleven
_landnotches_sep2016.pdf).

Bosetti, N. and Sims, S. (2016) *STOPPED: Why People Oppose
Residential Development in their Backyard.* London: Centre for
London (https://www.centreforlondon.org/publication/nim
by-opposition/).

Cheshire, P. (2009) Urban containment, housing affordability
and price stability – irreconcilable goals. SERC Policy Paper
No. 4. London School of Economics and Political Science
(http://eprints.lse.ac.uk/59240/).

Cheshire, P., Hilber, C. A. L. and Koster, H. R. A. (2018) Empty
homes, longer commutes: one of the many unintended consequences of more restrictive local planning. *Journal of Public
Economics* 158: 126–51 (http://eprints.lse.ac.uk/86441/13/
Cheshire_Empty-homes_Published.pdf). Original presentation delivered by Paul Cheshire at the Adam Smith Institute,
28 March (https://static1.squarespace.com/static/56eddde76
2cd9413e151ac92/t/5abd0887758d46f7ea637201/15223379
42910/PCC+28+03+2018+v01.pdf).

Global Property Guide (2017) World's most expensive cities
(https://www.globalpropertyguide.com/most-expensive
-cities).

Hilber, C. A. L. and Lyytikäinen, T. (2017) Transfer taxes and
household utility: distortion of the housing or labour market?
LSE Spatial Economics Research Centre, Discussion Paper
216 (http://personal.lse.ac.uk/hilber/hilber_wp/Hilber_Lyyti
kainen_forthcoming_JUE.pdf).

Hilber, C. A. L. and Turner, T. M. (2014) The Mortgage Interest De-
duction and its impact on home-ownership decisions. *Review*

*of Economics and Statistics* 96(4): 618–37 (http://eprints.lse .ac.uk/49843/1/Hilber_Mortgage_interest_deduction_2013 .pdf).

Hilber, C. A. L. and Vermeulen, W. (2016) The impact of supply constraints on house prices in England. *Economic Journal* 126(591): 358–405 (http://personal.lse.ac.uk/hilber/hilber_ wp/hilber_vermeulen_ej_forthcoming.pdf).

House of Lords Select Committee on Economic Affairs (2016) *Building More Homes.* London: House of Lords (https://pub lications.parliament.uk/pa/ld201617/ldselect/ldeconaf/ 20/20.pdf).

Hsieh, C.-T. and Moretti, E. (2018) Housing constraints and spa- tial misallocation. Paper w21154. Cambridge, MA: National Bureau of Economic Research (https://faculty.chicagobooth .edu/chang-tai.hsieh/research/growth.pdf).

KPMG (2008) Housebuilder annual reports. Housebuilding mar- ket study: study investigating financing for homebuilders.

Ministry of Housing, Communities and Local Government (2012) *Developing Farmland: Regulations on Land Use.* Lon- don: MHCLG (https://www.gov.uk/guidance/developing -farmland-regulations-on-land-use).

Ministry of Housing, Communities and Local Government (2018) *English Housing Survey 2016–17.* London: MHCLG (https://www.gov.uk/government/statistics/english-housing -survey-2016-to-2017-headline-report).

Mirrlees, J., Adam, S., Besley, T., Blundell, R., Bond, S., Chote, R., Gammie, M., Johnson, P., Myles, G. and Poterba, J. M. (2011) *Tax by Design.* London: Institute for Fiscal Studies (https:// www.ifs.org.uk/publications/mirrleesreview/).

Myers, J. (2017) The housing crisis: an act of devastating self harm. CapX, 11 August (https://capx.co/the-housing-crisis-an-act-of-devastating-economic-self-harm/).

Office for Budget Responsibility (2014) Forecasting house prices. Working Paper 6. London: OBR (http://obr.uk/docs/dlm_uploads/WorkingPaperNo6.pdf).

Office for National Statistics (2018) House price to workplace-based earnings ratio. Fareham: ONS (https://www.ons.gov.uk/peoplepopulationandcommunity/housing/datasets/ratioofhousepricetoworkplacebasedearningslowerquartileandmedian).

Office for National Statistics (2018) Housing affordability in England and Wales: 2017. Statistical Bulletin. Fareham: ONS (https://www.ons.gov.uk/peoplepopulationandcommunity/housing/bulletins/housingaffordabilityinenglandandwales/2017).

Papworth, T. (2016) *A Garden of One's Own: Suggestions for Development in the Metropolitan Green Belt*. London: Adam Smith Institute (https://www.adamsmith.org/research/a-garden-of-ones-own).

Sa, F. (2011) Immigration and house prices in the UK. IZA Discussion Paper 5893. Bonn: IZA (https://d-nb.info/1014192536/34).

Schumacher, P. (2018) *Only Capitalism Can Solve the Housing Crisis*. London: Adam Smith Institute (https://www.adamsmith.org/capitalismcansolvethehousingcrisis/).

# 5 PLANNING TO THE PEOPLE: HOW A SYSTEM OF TRANSFERABLE DEVELOPMENT RIGHTS COULD REPLACE THE GREEN BELT[1]

Thomas Schaffner

## Summary

The UK's housing shortage can best be characterised as a deficiency in supply arising from the high cost of development. A significant proportion of the cost can be attributed to the price of land, which is kept artificially high by planning measures such as the green belt. But comprehensive liberalisation of the land market is not politically viable at present. Given this, any policy fix needs to maintain the protected status of large swathes of green belt land, while simultaneously finding a way to increase the availability of buildable areas.

This essay proposes a system of 'transferable development rights' in response, which would essentially 'compensate' those affected by development on green belt land and could be used by local authorities to incentivise the construction of affordable accommodation. It also explores the housing crisis in greater detail, as well as

---

1   Student Prize Winner.

attempting to dispel some potential objections to this proposed reform.

## What is the housing crisis?

In the last forty years, house prices have increased by 4,300 per cent (Legal & General 2014). If wages had risen at the same rate, the average couple with children would earn an additional £44,000 a year and the average single person would earn an addition £29,000 per year (ibid.). As a result, the aspiration of owning one's own home seems totally out of reach to many of the school-leavers of today. In essence, these figures show that the housing crisis can be characterised as a dramatic increase in accommodation costs relative to the rise in wages.

Standard economic theory would dictate that a rapid surge in prices should be met with a corresponding increase in supply. Despite an abundance of land, though, the construction industry's response has been lacklustre. One explanation for this is that the high fixed costs of housebuilding make the supply of new homes inelastic, significantly dampening the effect of higher prices on total output. Another view is that planning restrictions and controls on the supply of land have contributed hugely to the expense associated with construction. The empirical evidence behind this second claim is strong. According to the ONS (2018), 72 per cent of the price of a new home can be attributed to the cost of the land. In 1995, it was 55 per cent. Ultimately, the supply of housing is contingent upon the supply of land, so ensuring that both markets operate effectively is imperative.

## The green belt

One of the most draconian aspects of UK planning law is the use of green belts around our towns and cities. Conceived in the post-war era of central planning, it was hoped that conserving chunks of countryside near major built-up areas would prevent 'urban sprawl' and safeguard England's green and pleasant land. Seventy years on, 13 per cent of English land is now designated as green belt on which development is essentially prohibited. The effect has been to stifle the natural outward growth of cities, restricting the supply of housing in the areas which require it the most. The great irony of the green belt is that, contrary to popular opinion, it is not exclusively made up of land which is of high environmental value or cultural significance. Some of it is already used for housing or public infrastructure; 35 per cent of it is used for intensive agriculture. In fact, it is estimated that 11 per cent of the UK's brownfield sites are on green belt land (Barker 2004). Simply put, arbitrarily deciding that land cannot be built on because of its proximity to another urban centre is not only illogical, it also has an incredibly distortionary effect on the property market. Given this, there is growing acceptance among economists that it is necessary to reform the restrictions on the supply of land.

## Framing the dilemma

Outlining these issues helps us to begin to characterise the type of reform which is economically sound. It should be clear that mustering the necessary political will to comprehensively liberalise green belt legislation would be a futile exercise. However, it is equally apparent that tackling the housing crisis will involve increasing the supply of land available for development. Any viable policy solution, though, will merely be an adaptation of existing rules.

It is worth pausing here to consider some of the arguments made in favour of the green belt to better understand what it is that people truly care about when they say they are in favour of its continued preservation. The popularly accepted line is that placing special protections on land around cities is necessary to prevent urban sprawl, conserve natural environments, and ensure the countryside retains an aesthetically desirable appearance. To an economist, though, these issues represent potential externalities associated with the development of housing. For instance, building homes may impose a cost on incumbent residents by spoiling their view. As Corkindale (2004) puts it, 'The environmental externalities associated with land development are, arguably, the main reason why land use planning policy is needed at all. Without them, there would be no real objection to allowing the market to determine how, where and when land is developed'.

It may seem obvious, but a thorough consideration of externalities is fundamental to anyone seeking to draft a potential reform to UK planning law. Even so, we have already established that green belt land is not as pristine as most people imagine it to be. The externality argument, therefore, is somewhat exaggerated. Despite this, by fully acknowledging the expressed concerns, we can avoid political pitfalls when framing a solution. If we accept that there is an externality associated with housebuilding, then we can focus our attention towards measures which seek to 'internalise' the social costs. Put simply, we need to find a way to compensate those affected by housing development to reflect the loss of welfare they endure.

## A market-based solution: 'transferable development rights'

Taking inspiration from a well-known method of pricing the externalities associated with pollution, transferable development rights (TDRs) seek to put a value on the cost of urban development. This is not a new idea and has been tested in certain parts of the US.

The scheme begins by 'zoning' the land available, dividing it between protected and unprotected zones. Sites of cultural significance and areas which are environmentally sensitive will belong to the former category, while the remaining land makes up the latter. Development rights are then assigned to landowners in the protected zones. These rights, however, can only be exercised in the unprotected zones. As a result, developers have to purchase these rights in order to obtain planning permission. Importantly, the TDRs are exhaustible and essentially give permanent protected status to the land from which they arise. Some schemes also dictate that planning restrictions can be relaxed if the developer is willing to purchase additional rights. In essence, this prices the external cost of construction and compensates landowners who have an interest in protecting the land around their property.

Clark and Downes (1996) looked at one of the most successful implementations of a TDR scheme. They wrote, 'The New Jersey Pinelands project is an important example of an innovative method that appears to have achieved community support for environmental protection while respecting ecological, economic, and cultural factors in land-use planning' (ibid.).

Emulating the features from successful projects such as this is necessary to ensure the reform achieves its objectives when applied to UK land policy. The Pinelands case study fulfils several conditions which set it apart from other trials. Firstly, there must be sufficient demand for development. Given the soaring price of new homes in the UK, one would hope this condition would be satisfied. Secondly, development must be able to cover the additional cost of the TDR. This is more of an unknown, as it is hard to say exactly what valuation landowners will place on their development rights. Despite this, the additional cost is not an issue as long as it offsets the downward effect on the price of land. Finally, the market for TDRs must be viable. In other words, buyers and sellers must be able to find each other and agree on a price.

In practice, many TDR schemes address this issue of market viability by making use of a 'credit bank' administered by the local authority. Its role is essentially to facilitate transactions between buyers and sellers. Moreover, this would allow local authorities to adopt a complementary policy, 'density transfer charges' (DTCs) (Pruetz 2016).

These would allow developers to 'top up' their development rights from the local authority, although this does not necessarily ensure that affected parties are fully compensated. DTCs have the advantage, though, of giving local decision makers flexibility over their local planning policy. As long as there is sufficient public oversight, this will enhance the democratic nature of the new planning system. It also addresses instances where there is 'common' land which has no legal owner.

## A replacement for the green belt?

The policy proposal involves adapting this idea to make it appropriate for application to the green belt, and, more generally, to the UK's housing shortage. Implementation would begin, as described above, by zoning protected land. A significant proportion will of course be preserved, especially if it is already designated as an Area of Outstanding Natural Beauty. Additionally, agricultural land could also be given special protected status, as would sites of important cultural significance. Once such areas have been identified, we would be left with land that is deemed acceptable for development. Importantly, significant control over which land should be preserved would be given to local councils, either at district or parish level. Only if local authorities proved reluctant to liberalise would central government impose a requirement to free up certain land. However, the aim should be to devolve as much power over planning control as possible. Communities are the best judges of their own interests and are ideally placed to decide which land should be conserved and which has low environmental value. More fundamentally, local oversight might be necessary to make these reforms politically palatable.

TDRs are then allocated to landowners in the protected areas or held in trust by the local authority if the land is unowned. To build in the development zones, one would need to obtain a TDR. The effect of the right would be to liberalise the planning restrictions facing the developer. By purchasing additional rights, developers would be allowed to pursue more elaborate construction projects. For instance, they would be able to build at higher densities or to a greater height. This would open up the opportunity of development on green belt land while disincentivising highly disruptive construction.

Responsibility for the administration of the TDR scheme would be given to local authorities, who would operate a credit bank system as mentioned above. This would also allow councils to release additional rights (or density transfer charges, as we have called them) to meet local needs. For example, one of the most talked about aspects of the housing crisis is the lack of affordable new homes. Authorities would be able to use the TDR system as a way to reward or punish developers for their performance against this objective by granting additional rights to those who have a track record of producing high-quality, low-cost dwellings. In essence, TDRs give councils a market-based instrument to encourage the construction of homes for which there is the greatest need.

What is the political advantage of this scheme? We have already discussed how the relinquishment of land zoning control to local authorities adds a democratic aspect to a TDR system. On top of this, though, the marketisation of planning rights is essentially a quid pro quo for liberalising green belt land. After all, we can assume that part of the value of existing property in these areas is attributable to its protected status. Therefore, a case could be made that property owners should be compensated for any significant changes to the planning system. As Pruetz (2016) puts it, 'these programs offer [TDRs] as a gesture of fairness to the owners of properties subject to restrictions designed to protect certain community benefits such as prime farmland or sensitive watersheds'. From an economic point of view, TDRs also internalise the externalities of development by placing a price on the social cost of housebuilding. Moreover, reallocating this expense to those affected enhances the optimality of the land reform: everyone is either as well off as, or better off than, they were before. Overall, TDRs create an economic incentive for land market liberalisation, making it sufficiently politically appealing.

## Potential criticisms

Adding an additional cost to the development of land in order to bring down house prices seems counter-intuitive. Surely we want to make housebuilding as cheap as possible. As we have already seen, however, a substantial proportion of the cost of new homes is accounted for by the price of the land. Although charging a fee for planning rights would be an additional expense, this would only have an adverse effect on housing supply if the cost were greater than the simultaneous fall in the price of land as green belt areas are liberalised.

In response to this, some might argue that a more effective solution would be to just declassify the green belt without commodifying planning rights. And they would be correct. As we have already established, though, this is politically impossible. TDRs help us to circumvent the widespread opposition one might expect by compensating those with a vested interest in protecting the green belt. More fundamentally, under a TDR scheme development is contingent upon the permanent conservation of land in specified zones. Returning planning rights to individuals is a method by which we can properly enshrine this in law.

## Conclusion

Unlocking the supply of land is a necessary step to fix the housing crisis. As a result, a policy solution needs to make the liberalisation of land supply publicly appealing, while also conforming to economic logic. Applying a system of transferable development rights to the green belt would achieve just this. From an economic perspective, such a policy would internalise the externalities associated with development. It would also be politically appealing: those most vigorously opposed to green belt reform would stand to gain. In brief, the TDR scheme would apply the principles of voluntary exchange to planning permission.

# References

Barker, K. (2004) *Review of Housing Supply (Final Report – Recommendations)*. London: HMSO (http://news.bbc.co.uk/nol/shared/bsp/hi/pdfs/17_03_04_barker_review.pdf).

Clark, D. and Downes, D. (1996) What price biodiversity economic incentives and biodiversity conservation in the United States. *Journal of Environmental Law and Litigation* 11(1): 9–89.

Corkindale, J. (2004) *The Land Use Planning System*. London: Institute of Economic Affairs.

Legal & General (2014) *Let's House Britain*. London: Legal & General (https://www.legalandgeneralgroup.com/media/1091/lets_house_britain.pdf).

Office for National Statistics (2018) National Accounts 2018, National Balance Sheet (https://www.ons.gov.uk/economy/grossdomesticproductgdp/compendium/unitedkingdomnationalaccountsthebluebook/2018/supplementarytables).

Pruetz, R. (2016) Eco-cities and transferable development credits. *Eco-Cities Reflections* 1(18): 1–15.

# 6 TAKING ON ESTABLISHED INTERESTS: A NEW APPROACH TO LAND TO SOLVE THE HOUSING SHORTAGE[1]

William Watts and Luke McWatters

## Summary

Inflated land prices due to years of artificial restrictions on supply are at the core of our housing woes. As land now makes up the majority of the cost of new housing, tackling this issue is at the heart of addressing high prices, as well as creating space for new construction.

The proposed Land and Liberty Act would remove the designation of green belt completely, freeing up land for development in areas of high value and high demand around major urban centres. Meanwhile, it would maintain picturesque areas by extending Areas of Outstanding Natural Beauty (AONBs).

Planning permission rules create unnecessary barriers to entry for smaller construction firms and restrict the overall supply of land for housing, driving up prices. The Land and Liberty Act will loosen and streamline these

---

1   School Prize Winner.

rules, particularly for changing land use on agricultural land towards construction.

Agricultural subsidies restrict large swathes of land to inefficient use. As the UK leaves the European Union (EU), the Act will withdraw all such subsidies in five years. This will incentivise farmers in areas of high housing demand to sell off land to developers and lead to an increase in the housing stock.

## The problem of UK land use

Land prices in the UK are out of control. Fifty years ago, total UK land values amounted to around 50 per cent of GDP; now they are worth 200 per cent (Schumacher 2018). Land prices have been driven up by state-imposed restrictions on supply, backed up by entrenched political interests defending the status quo. This rise in the price of land has been transferred directly to housing, with land now making up most of the cost of new constructions. At present, the primary barrier to homeownership is the high price of housing itself. Since 1997, house prices have grown by around 6 per cent annually, twice as fast as earnings (Hamptons International 2016: 7). The result of this is long-term renting and a gradual increase in the median age of first-time buyers. To increase the number and proportion of property owners, the ever-increasing gap between earnings and house prices must be reduced. Tackling our land problem is the most effective way of doing this.

Our proposal, the Land and Liberty Act, gets to the heart of the issue of land. The Act will push away the system of command economics which has restricted housing supply and forced up house prices for decades. The initiative has three parts, which together will move land use towards housing, and help lower house prices to increase homeownership.

The first part is removing the designation of vast swathes of valuable land around urban areas as green belt, opening up opportunities for building where housing is most in demand. The second part will loosen and streamline the planning system, particularly with regard to changing land use towards housebuilding on agricultural land. This will encourage the freeing up of land while still maintaining individual choice for landowners. The third part will complement the loosening of planning on agricultural land. This will be through a gradual, but total, withdrawal of agricultural subsidies to realign land towards its most productive purposes. Due to excess demand for homes, a freer market will see land use move towards housing. By parting with a dysfunctional set of interventionist rules and principles on land, this initiative will give the market the space it needs to deliver for the future of housing and our society.

## Re-evaluation of green belt designated land

Green belts strangle the most productive areas of our country by restricting the supply of housing near where demand is highest. This directly contributes to a lack of housing stock and inflated prices within and around the urban areas themselves. Furthermore, the reality is that much of the UK's green belt is not as idyllic as depicted by countryside campaigners and the media. The special designation of this land by the government has become increasingly harmful and wasteful over the policy's lifetime, with the negatives of restricted housing supply now clearly outweighing the benefits.

The Land and Liberty Act would remove the designation of any UK land as green belt. This will unleash housebuilding by construction companies eager to capitalise on areas of extremely high demand and profitability on the edge of major cities. The potential for increased housing stock is astounding. In London, where the green belt is an absurd three times the size of the city it encloses (Mace et al. 2016: 20), research suggests that just 3.7 per cent of this land could accommodate one million homes (Adam Smith Institute 2015). Greenfield sites also make up most of this land. They are far cheaper to build on than brownfield sites mostly located in central urban areas. Fear of construction on greenfield land is misplaced. Greenfield land offers cheaper production costs for firms as, unlike brownfield land, there is no need for expensive land use changes or clean-up operations on the site. Therefore, greenfield land offers a valuable opportunity to keep housing costs down, making it more accessible and giving more people the ability to buy newly constructed properties rather than just rent.

The political challenge of reforming the green belt is enormous. To increase this policy's viability, areas will be preserved with the extension of the Areas of Outstanding Natural Beauty (AONB) designation. Some areas already possess this, such as the Surrey Hills, which lie to the south of London's green belt. This will quell some concerns, while still providing a massive boost to the housing stock. The market will be able to step in to satisfy the huge demand around many of the country's cities, including London, Oxford and Cambridge, which are affected by centrally imposed restrictions dating back to the 1940s. This will markedly reduce the housing shortage in these highly populated regions and thus, by extension, in the country as a whole.

## Reforming the system of planning

The current web of planning conditions and permissions is antiquated and draconian. It is a clear cause of inflated house prices and supply shortages. The cost of land with planning compared with agricultural land demonstrates this problem. The weighted average price of one hectare of land with residential planning permission is around £6 million, compared with a mere £21,000 for one hectare of a typical agricultural site (DCLG 2015). This is an outrageous situation, emblematic of the artificial constraints placed on the housing supply.

The Land and Liberty Act will significantly loosen and streamline planning permission rules. In particular, the initiative will make a change in land use much more easily achievable on agricultural land. In tandem with the removal of agricultural subsidies, this will help allow those who farm in areas of high housing demand, such as green belts, to change land use towards construction: the land can then be sold off by its owners for significant profits. With this incentive in place, houses are more likely to be built where they are most needed. Where housing is most in demand, there will exist a greater enticement for farmers to change land use due to the potential for gains. Housebuilding should then see significant improvements in regions where supply is failing to meet current demand.

The planning changes in the Land and Liberty Act will lead not only to a greater stock of housing but also an increased number and proportion of property owners. With planning much easier to obtain, the cost of land with planning should fall significantly due to increased supply. This means cheaper costs of production for construction companies, lowering housing costs and increasing scope for individuals on lower incomes to take out mortgages. Furthermore, streamlined planning rules will increase competition by enabling smaller firms to operate more easily in the market. The economist Michael Ball explains the advantages larger construction firms possess in a planning environment such as exists at present: 'larger enterprises have employee skill-bases, capital-bases and land banks that enable them to spread risks, lower financing costs, improve negotiating positions with land-owners and facilitate strategic actions' (Ball 2003: 909).

Simpler planning rules will therefore reduce the advantages big companies currently have in negotiating power with the authorities. This will lower barriers to entry in the housing market and increase competition. With smaller firms more easily able to operate in the new conditions established, larger construction companies will be less able to exploit their market power. This will drive down prices of new housing, boosting affordability and thus homeownership.

## The removal of agricultural subsidies

The current agricultural subsidy regime is a perfect example of 'an unholy coalition of the do-gooders on the one hand and the special interests on the other' (Heffner and Friedman 1975), who come together to reduce market efficiency. The EU's Common Agricultural Policy (CAP) has an impact on the agricultural sector that is well established: reduced competition and inefficient farms shielded from market forces. However, what is not often considered is its negative effect on the land supply of the UK and the knock-on effect this has on housing costs.

The CAP creates perverse incentives that are damaging to both the housing market and the overall economy. At present an estimated 42 per cent of farms would make a loss without these subsidies (*The Economist* 2018), which suggests that an excess of land is occupied by (a minority of) unproductive farms. Part of the solution to increasing housebuilding and reducing its shortage lies in freeing up this land, and, once freed, this land will help reduce the biggest single cost of new houses. It is therefore vital that, upon the UK's departure from the EU, these subsidies are discontinued.

The Land and Liberty Act proposes the total abolition of agricultural subsidies over five years. This will streamline the agricultural sector by boosting the efficiency of remaining farms. Through this process, the inevitable closure of a number of inefficient farms will create space for new housing projects, undoing the unintended damage the subsidies have wreaked on the housing market. The previously mentioned disparity between the low cost of agricultural land compared with land with planning creates an incentive for inefficient farms near urban centres to convert to residential areas. The phasing out of agricultural subsidies will help to restore a free market in land, which will stabilise at an equilibrium where enough housing is provided and high output farms remain. Since the main barrier to homeownership is the high price of housing itself, the increased supply of land should reduce prices and increase the number of people able to buy housing.

## Political considerations

The gap between what is politically possible and what is economically necessary has often put politicians off enacting structural reforms. In the case of the housing shortage, such hesitation is unnecessary.

One potential challenge to this initiative is that, since around 65 per cent of households are owner-occupiers (Barton 2017: 3), any policy that sees house prices fall, or even stop increasing, could be viewed as politically unfeasible. However, once the long-term interests of property owners are taken into account, it becomes clear that a slowdown in house prices would benefit many people. Data released by the Office for National Statistics show that the percentage of young adults living with their parents in the

UK has risen from 21 per cent in 1996 to 26 per cent in 2017, rising from 2.7 million to 3.4 million in the last two decades (Bulman 2017). If this problem remains unresolved, many parents will have to pay large sums to help purchase their children's first homes. Furthermore, most owner-occupiers do not intend to sell the property on which they have spent many years paying off a mortgage. If we truly wish to rejuvenate our property-owning democracy, young people must be able to become independent homeowners, and a stabilisation of house prices is the only way of achieving this.

Another challenge may be that the withdrawal of the subsidies to agriculture is politically difficult. However, enacting the policies prescribed by the Land and Liberty Act actually offers many farmers an opportunity to benefit. As outlined, the combination of subsidy removal and the easing of planning restrictions on changing land use will allow farmers to sell their land for a significant profit. With the lifting of regulations, the land will easily be converted into housing, meaning that many farmers will be well compensated. However, there will inevitably be some who are both inefficient and located away from areas of high housing demand. For these, the five-year withdrawal period will allow for long-term planning to deal with the subsidy removal and offer the opportunity to make changes to farming practices.

Furthermore, historical precedent exists for the subsidy removal. In 1984, New Zealand abolished almost all of its agricultural subsidies in a period of twelve months. Although in the short run this caused uncertainty and low capital investment, in the long run the policy was a resounding success. Providing an extended phase-out period would minimise these impacts on investment and certainty. The Land and Liberty Act therefore offers a solution that is good for the housing sector but also fair to farmers.

## Conclusion

Reforming the UK's policy on land is the closest thing there is to a silver bullet that can solve the housing crisis. If the system is not reformed, the continuation of current housing trends is inevitable. This means further rises in the median age of first-time buyers, real increases in house prices, and a declining proportion of property owners. The Land and Liberty Act paves the way for markets in land and housing to transform the situation. It is a bold stand against overzealous centralised planning which dates back to the 1940s and against the regulations that have disastrously restricted supply and inflated house prices. The initiative will free up land, giving the market the space to build houses where they are needed. With intensified competition, downward pressure on house prices will lower the biggest barrier to owning a home in Britain today. The three parts of this initiative will come together to fundamentally shift the balance of power towards the many young families and individuals struggling to find an affordable home. In the long term, it will inject new energy into our democracy by reopening the valuable opportunity of homeownership.

# References

Adam Smith Institute (2015) Free up 3.7 percent of London's Green Belt to build one million new homes, says new report. Press release (https://www.adamsmith.org/news/press-relea se-free-up-3-7-percent-of-londons-green-belt-to-build-one -million-new-homes-says-new-report).

Ball, M. (2003) Markets and the structure of the housebuilding industry: an international perspective. *Urban Studies* 40(5–6): 897–916.

Barton, C. (2017) *Home Ownership and Renting: Demographics*. London: House of Commons Library (https://research briefings.parliament.uk/ResearchBriefing/Summary/CBP -7706#fullreport).

Bulman, M. (2017) Number of young adults living with parents reaches record high. *The Independent*, 8 November (https:// www.independent.co.uk/news/uk/home-news/young-ad ults-live-parents-at-home-property-buy-homeowners-hous ing-market-a8043891.html).

DCLG (2015) *Land Value Estimates for Policy Appraisal*. London: Department for Communities and Local Government (https://assets.publishing.service.gov.uk/government/up loads/system/uploads/attachment_data/file/407155/Feb ruary_2015_Land_value_publication_FINAL.pdf).

*Economist* (2018) A new furrow: the future of the countryside. *The Economist*, 1 September.

Hamptons International (2016) *Measuring the Deposit Barrier*. London: Hamptons International (hamptonsinternational-fo cusreport-timetosave-spring.pdf).

Heffner, R. and Friedman, M. (1975) Living within our means. TV interview. The Open Mind, 7 December. New York: WPIX, Channel 11.

Mace, A., Blanc, F., Gordon, I. and Scanlon, K. (2016) A 21st century metropolitan green belt. LSE Knowledge Exchange (http://www.lse.ac.uk/geography-and-environment/assets/Documents/Green-Belt-Report.pdf).

Schumacher, P. (2018) *Only Capitalism Can Solve the Housing Crisis*. London: Adam Smith Institute (https://www.adamsmith.org/capitalismcansolvethehousingcrisis/).

# 7 THE LOCALISM 2.0 REFORM

Gintas Vilkelis

## Summary

There are several obstacles in the way of new housing construction, of which local opposition to new housing projects is the hardest to overcome, because no market-based mechanisms are available for meaningfully compensating the current residents for the financial downside and inconvenience caused by new housing.

The Localism 2.0 reform would enable local authorities to operate much more like independent businesses (i.e. with much greater freedom to earn money and to decide how best to spend it). This would make a market-based compensation mechanism eminently possible and would result in a large increase in the number of houses built, increasing the number and proportion of property owners in the UK. Market testing indicates that this reform would receive a high degree of support in Parliament and be embraced by the country.

## The problem

There are several obstacles to new housing construction:

- Local opposition to new housing projects (Nimbyism).
- Difficulties for local authorities in obtaining the funds needed for housebuilding.
- Lack of a self-build tradition, which among other things leads to house construction in this country being dominated by a small number of large companies.
- 'Land banking' by the aforementioned large companies to maximise profits, etc.

The biggest (and hardest to overcome) of these obstacles is local opposition among *current* residents to new housing projects. The reason for this opposition is quite simple: in the vast majority of cases the proposed new construction brings no benefit to existing residents, only cost and inconvenience (reducing the capital appreciation potential of their homes, causing more traffic, less tranquillity, more crowded local schools and GP surgeries, etc.).

Given the above considerations, why would anybody not be opposed to new construction near where they live? Even though a gradually increasing number of current homeowners realise that their opposition to new development in their area might make it almost impossible for their children and grandchildren to buy their own homes, the societal benefits of more housebuilding are somewhat nebulous, spread country-wide and 'sometime in the future', while the costs to them of building 'in their backyard' are specific, direct and immediate.

What is currently missing is a politically permitted market mechanism whereby current residents would be directly and tangibly compensated for the downsides to them of housebuilding nearby. Such a market-based mechanism would dramatically reduce local opposition to new housing projects.

This new mechanism will firstly have to be able to compensate (or even reward when possible) the current residents in tangible ways for the cost and inconvenience of new housing, and secondly mitigate the negatives which cannot be adequately compensated for by the former.

The first objective can be accomplished mainly via the combination of, firstly, direct financial benefits (especially to the residents who would be the most directly and tangibly affected by new housing) through sizeable reductions in taxes levied on them or sometimes possibly even through cash payments, and secondly the improvement in local government services that new housing would make possible due to an increased local tax base (i.e. new residents).

The second objective would be achieved by making sure that part of the new revenue associated with new housing developments would be used to upgrade and augment local infrastructure (schools, GP surgeries, etc.), so that an increase in the local population need not cause, or further exacerbate, shortages.

Moreover, local opposition to new housing developments can be further reduced if current residents are given enough say in the aesthetic design and layout of new developments. Under the current system, local decisions on architectural design issues can be implemented immediately (and indeed are already being implemented quite successfully in a number of areas), though obtaining adequate funding for upgrading and scaling up local infrastructure often falters. Meanwhile, compensating or rewarding residents financially is not feasible, because in the UK approximately 95 per cent of taxes go straight to Westminster while local councils are permanently cash-strapped.

Metaphorically, under the current highly centralised system, local authorities operate like departments of a large and inefficient, internal-politics-driven corporation, whereby each (highly disempowered) department is given a fixed and inflexible 'annual budget' and is told what it must do, regardless of whether the distant CEO's orders make sense or not.

## The policy vision

The political reform that would properly address all the problems above must necessarily be centred on the meaningful fiscal (and also regulatory) empowerment of local councils, so that they have the necessary powers, flexibility and resources to react quickly to changing circumstances, and do what they know is right and needs to be done.

In practical terms, this means that local authorities (county and below) should be allowed to operate much more like independent businesses, whereby they have freedom and flexibility to decide how to earn money and how to spend it in the best way possible (just like all 'normal' businesses routinely do).

Under this paradigm, the primary mission of the local councils would be redefined. They would no longer be the disempowered 'implementation units' of central government's decisions and policies. Instead they would be free to make the best use of land for the benefit of their residents.

Local councils will be dealing with (and will seek to please) the following three groups of people:

- Paying customers (tax-paying residents and businesses).
- Investors (in cases where, for example, councils need to borrow money for major infrastructure projects – including building new houses).
- 'Shareholders' (all the residents of the area the council controls, because, unlike in the case of a 'proper' company, the 'shareholding' in this case will be defined by residency and not by investment, and hence will democratically represent the interests of residents).

This way, executives will have the necessary powers, resources and flexibility to do what is necessary to attract and keep 'paying customers' (i.e. residents and businesses) by making the area a desirable place to live (via low taxes and well-administered public services) and by creating a business-friendly environment (low taxes, sensible and benign regulations, availability of qualified employees living in the area).

The role of the councillors would be to be the 'eyes and ears' in each local area (thus democratically representing the voices of residents) and to sit on the 'board of directors' that would keep the (hired) executives accountable and informed about everything happening in their area that might require their action.

This scheme brings the best features and practices of markets (that have made private enterprise so successful) into the field of government, while increasing the degree of democratic representation of the interests of everyone living in the area. Compared with the current system (centred on national government), residents will have much easier access to their representatives, and local executives will have much greater flexibility to react to emerging problems and opportunities.

In a nutshell, this proposal is a form of radical devolution that will shift most of the taxation (and a significant amount of regulation) from the national to the local level, so that instead of 95 per cent of all taxes collected going straight to central government, most will be collected locally.

Broadly, the best example to follow is Switzerland, where a typical resident pays about 40 per cent of their taxes to their 'commune' (the town/parish equivalent), about 40 per cent to their canton (the county equivalent) and only about 20 per cent to the federal government in Bern (most of it through VAT and excise taxes). The top marginal personal income tax rate in most localities is in the mid 20 per cent range (compared with 45 per cent in the UK). Despite being poor in natural resources, Switzerland is one of the most prosperous countries in the world, and its high degree of localism may partly explain this.

This policy solution is termed 'Localism 2.0' to differentiate it from the 'Localism Act of 2011', which, while a step in the right direction, stopped far short of what is needed. The more comprehensive definition of Localism 2.0 is that decisions should be made as closely as possible to the people they affect. Therefore only the functions that can (arguably) be performed most effectively at national level (foreign policy, defence, border control, etc.) should remain with central government, while the rest of the fiscal and regulatory powers should be shifted from Westminster to local councils (county and below).

## Increasing the number of houses built and the proportion of property owners

Localism 2.0 will lead to a substantial increase in the rate of housebuilding by directly addressing the main obstacles listed at the beginning of this paper. Local opposition to new housing projects will be dramatically reduced because, under Localism 2.0, councils will have the fiscal tools and resources both to properly compensate current residents for the cost and inconvenience caused by the new houses built next to them, and to properly upgrade local infrastructure to cope with increased demand due to increased population.

As for local public discussions on the aesthetic design and layout of the new developments, under Localism 2.0 these will become even more common than they are now, thus reducing Nimby opposition even further. And as far as local authorities have difficulty in obtaining funds needed due to housebuilding, this problem will be largely eliminated because councils will have much greater access to financial resources (both via increased taxation powers and ability to borrow from investors).

As for the lack of competition in the building industry, newly empowered local councils will have vast powers to encourage self-builders and smaller builders, thus breaking up the current unhealthy monopoly of a few large building companies. The resulting competition would help to reverse the house price trend, making the practice of 'land banking' less profitable for the big firms.

Unaffordable house prices are caused by a housing shortage. Once this has been addressed, the market's supply and demand mechanism will inevitably cause house prices to decline to more affordable levels, which will cause an increase in the number and proportion of property owners in the UK.

## Why reform would be possible

The reason Localism 2.0 would be so compelling to so many people is because once the systemic root causes of the major problems have been explained, then the solution becomes more or less self-evident.

Localism 2.0 also has a strong appeal to emotion. It addresses the widening dichotomy between the degree of choice and control people experience in their commercial lives (where we can satisfy desires instantly, or nearly so, through the likes of Amazon, Uber, Netflix, etc.), and the lack of control over unresolved and serious problems that the state has perpetually been in charge of fixing – housing being a prime example. Given that most laws in this country are 'one size fits all' and imposed nationally, this means most people are powerless to change them, even when they think they make no sense.

People have been growing unhappy with this situation and have expressed their displeasure by voting for anti-establishment candidates and ideas. Even though this dichotomy is stronger than ever, it is by no means new: it was genuine empowerment that was the secret of the 'Right to Buy' policy of the 1980s. As Michael Heseltine noted then, this 'reversed the trend of ever-increasing dominance of the state over the life of the individual' and consequently 'no single piece of legislation had enabled the transfer of so much capital wealth from the state to the people'.[1] To rephrase Michael Heseltine's quote, Localism 2.0 will reverse the trend of ever-increasing dominance of the state over the life of the individual, and no single piece of legislation will enable the transfer of so much power from the state to the people. Localism 2.0 constitutes a genuine embodiment of empowerment.

---

1   Housing Bill, HC Deb, 15 January 1980: 976(1443-575) (https://api.parlia ment.uk/historic-hansard/commons/1980/jan/15/housing-bill).

# 8 A SUPPLY-SIDE ANSWER TO THE HOUSING CRISIS: FALSE IMPRESSIONS AND TRUE SOLUTIONS

Calvin Chan

## Summary

This essay begins by challenging the general perception that the housing crisis is essentially caused by an increase in demand which the market has no way of meeting. It presents arguments as to why this is a false impression, setting the stage for the argument for a supply-side solution. Before presenting that case, it goes through a number of tried-and-failed remedies, many of which focus too directly on dealing with affordability. This is a mistake, since it treats the symptoms without curing the disease, which in this case is the undersupply of land. The essay concludes by recommending some adjustments to the institutional arrangements which have distorted the housing market, and offers some suggestions as to how to pacify Nimby sentiments, such that efforts to expand the stock of housing can be pursued in a way that is politically viable in the long run.

## Introduction

This essay was written in the conviction that the shortage of supply is the primary cause of the housing crisis and that the most straightforward solution consists in expanding the stock of housing available.

Polls reveal that most of the British public reject this analysis. According to one survey in 2016, more than half believe immigration to be the main contributor to the crisis, apparently driving up demand to a point that supply cannot match (Tigar 2016). Given this indifference to shortage of supply as a diagnosis of the problem, many tend also to be sceptical of supply-side solutions, preferring instead to stem demand as a method of tackling the issue.

A broadly supply-oriented solution must overcome the widely held views summarised above. The challenge is, in a way, twofold: for the public to take on this kind of solution to the crisis, they must first be 'on board' with a particular understanding of its causes. This essay therefore begins with some arguments as to why the general perception is not in fact accurate, and that the problem of housing is indeed a problem of supply. It then identifies some areas of policy that can realistically be adjusted in order to build up the stock of housing available. This, however, is tricky, and steps must be taken to mitigate the concerns that provoke opposition to building. The remainder of the essay argues for a series of changes in the regulatory regime that would alleviate the shortage. The aim is to increase the supply of low-density housing on green belt land, while restructuring fiscal incentives to encourage more extensive approvals of residential development.

## The causes of the current crisis

To begin with, it should be recognised that the current scarcity is largely artificial. It is of course true that the supply of land is finite: but the reason there is no shortage of fish or wood is not because they are somehow inexhaustible, but down to the policies adopted, which determine the extent of their availability.

It is revealing to compare, for example, the number of houses built barely a generation ago, to the figures today. Fifty years ago, 352,540 new-build dwellings were completed in England (MHCLG n.d.). By contrast, the same figure for 2017 was 163,200, less than half what was managed in 1968 (ibid.). Why the dramatic drop?

One explanation is that the country has simply run out of space, and that the dearth of supply is due to physical limits. This is not supported by any hard data, while there is in fact a good deal of evidence that the complex regulatory regime is the real villain. One authoritative study, which supports this claim, isolates the impact of regulatory barriers on the supply of housing, independent of natural obstacles (i.e. scarcity of land and topographical constraints). It finds that, while these latter constraints had been decisive elsewhere (e.g. Massachusetts), their effects had been limited in the English context (Hilber and Vermeulen 2016).

These findings are not novel, and they are well-known to those familiar with the housing debate. Nevertheless, for supply-side solutions to have political purchase, the public must first be brought around to the correct diagnosis of what caused the crisis in the first place. Unlike most political issues, there is no shortage of political will, on both the left and right, to meet the challenge posed by housing. However, the debate appears to be stuck, in part because there is a good deal of misunderstanding of the problem and its causes.

## The wrong kind of solution

Once it is recognised that a dearth of supply is the cause of the crisis, the obvious next step is to get to work on expanding the supply available. Here, it is important to identify the right remedy, and set aside strategies that either have not worked or will not work.

Help to Buy is one example of a largely wrong-headed approach, which seeks to assist buyers directly by, essentially, giving them money. This kind of scheme has been implemented in a number of places. Take Singapore, for example, which dealt with down-payment difficulties using an inventive arrangement whereby first-time buyers were allowed to dip into their pension.[1] The London Borough of Newham has been keen to set up a comparable scheme.[2] The trouble

---

1 'Workers were allowed to use their accumulated CPF [Central Provident Fund] savings to pay the percent down payment and service the housing loan for the balance by monthly instalments over years' (Lee 2000: 96).

2 'In the London Borough of Newham discussions are under way with the Mill Group about the prospect of using the local authority's pension fund to invest in the Investors in Housing fund, co-investing with people looking to buy their first home, enabling them to move from the rented sector,

with these initiatives is that, unless the current rationing of land is overturned, demand will continue to outstrip supply. Directly increasing funds available to buyers merely signals to sellers that people can now pay more, which exacerbates the problem by inflating prices further.

Similar criticisms apply to efforts to reduce the cost of construction. Off-site manufacturing, for instance, has been touted as an alternative to traditional (and expensive) building methods. It is meant to relieve shortages by reducing production costs[3] (other ideas include the use of 3D printed houses, and the first such project is already under way in the Netherlands (Heathman 2018)). But such proposals cannot be expected to make much difference unless they are coupled with a vast increase in the supply of land. Demand would continue to exceed what the market can provide, with the predictable result that the limited output will go to the highest bidders.

## The right kind of solution

The focus, therefore, should be on the supply of land. This is the key to increasing the number of houses available, and by extension the number of property owners in the UK. In what follows, a two-pronged approach is set out, concentrating on areas where there is the most room for realistic adjustments.

---

or from living at home with their parents, sooner than they would otherwise have been able to do' (Hull et al. 2011).

3   The Science and Technology Select Committee has recommended this method as a potential solution (House of Lords 2018).

Perhaps the most promising way of increasing the supply of land is to abolish the current incentive structure, which discourages government agencies from granting the necessary permissions for housing in any given area. Take Stamp Duty. Right now, the heavily centralised tax system means that Local Planning Authorities do not stand to benefit from approving residential projects, since they do not get to keep the money generated. In a report titled 'Building More Homes', the House of Lords Select Committee on Economic Affairs admits that 'there is currently no immediate financial benefit to the local authority from the planning process. The "windfall" created by the grant of planning permission is retained by the landowner' (House of Lords 2016). In addition, local authorities may be left to address the downsides of development, such as increased congestion on transport networks and additional strains on the local school system. These problems can also be expected to anger residents.

This situation is clearly not conducive to more extensive building and reinforces the undersupply of land. Devolution of development-related taxes will go some way towards correcting this distorted incentive structure, where it pays to refuse permission to build. The revenue that comes with development should be retained by the relevant locality, such that permitting development becomes a means for local authorities to expand their tax base, and so they are at least financially compensated (Niemietz 2015).

It is also vital to look for ways of softening any backlash, and this section ends with some thoughts on how to avoid the kind of dogged opposition to new development seen in recent years. One issue worth examining is the type of housing that should be built in the efforts to increase supply. Objections often focus on the way housebuilding projects negatively affect the visual character of a given locale. The very name of the Campaign to Protect Rural England reveals the deep affection many have for the countryside and illustrates the nature of their concern about large-scale residential development.

One way of reducing this kind of opposition is to opt for building the sort of homes that are least likely to damage local scenery. This may mean low-density homes of a kind that fit in with the existing stock of housing in an area, as opposed to the high-rise apartment blocks that governments often seem to prefer. While high-density blocks of flats may provide more 'bang for the buck', this kind of approach may undermine the political support needed for a lasting solution to the housing crisis.

There are, moreover, major downsides from high-density housing. According to a Create Streets report, new homes across Europe are on average 6 per cent larger than existing homes. In France, Denmark and Germany, those figures are 20, 19 and 16 per cent respectively (Smith and Toms 2018). By contrast, the UK is somewhat unique by European standards in that new homes tend to be smaller than existing ones, which goes some way towards explaining the initially puzzling preference the British people have for older homes. Finally, the overwhelming preference of the public is to own homes with gardens rather than flats in high-rise apartment blocks, so it may not be wise to address the housing crisis by building a large number of homes in which people do not want to live (Smith and Toms 2018: 14–15).

## Conclusion

This essay has presented the case for a supply-side solution to the housing crisis. It has shown that the shortage of supply is the primary cause of the crisis and that the most straightforward solution consists of expanding the stock of housing available. The evidence for the former is compelling and the academic literature on the topic supports this claim. Institutional arrangements should be reformed so that regulatory bodies can more reliably supply an amount of land that meets demand. Moreover, the concerns of those opposed to development should be addressed. The proposals outlined would hopefully overcome the political stalemate that has thus far prevented a resolution of Britain's most urgent crisis.

## References

Heathman, A. (2018) 3D printed houses are coming and you could live in one from next year. *Evening Standard*, 6 June (https://www.standard.co.uk/tech/3d-printed-houses-neth erlands-project-milestone-a3857031.html).

Hilber, C. A. L. and Vermeulen, W. (2016) The impact of supply constraints on house prices in England. *Economic Journal* 126(591): 358–405.

Hull, A., Cooke, G. and Dolphin, T. (2011) *Build Now or Pay Later? Funding New Housing Supply*. London: Institute for Public Policy Research.

House of Lords (2016) Building more homes. Select Committee on Economic Affairs, 1st Report of Session 2016–17. London: House of Lords (https://publications.parliament.uk/pa/ld 201617/ldselect/ldeconaf/20/20.pdf).

House of Lords (2018) Off-site manufacture for construction: building for change. Science and Technology Select Committee, 2nd Report of Session 2017–19. London: House of Lords (https://publications.parliament.uk/pa/ld201719/ldselect/ ldsctech/169/169.pdf).

Lee, K. Y. (2000) *From Third World to First – The Singapore Story. 1965–2000*. New York: Harper Collins.

MHCLG (n.d.) Table 244: House building: permanent dwellings started and completed, by tenure. London: Ministry of Housing, Communities and Local Government (https://www.gov .uk/government/uploads/system/uploads/attachment_data/ file/720262/LiveTable244.xlsx).

Niemietz, K. (2015) *Reducing Poverty Through Policies to Cut the Cost of Living*. York: Joseph Rowntree Foundation.

Smith, N. B. and Toms, K. (2018) *From Nimby to Yimby: How to Win Votes by Building More Homes*. London: Create Streets (http://dev.createstreets.com/wp-content/uploads/2018/04/ Nimby-to-Yimby-280418.pdf).

Tigar, D. (2016) UK housing crisis: poll reveals city v country split on who to blame. *The Guardian*, 30 April (https:// www.theguardian.com/cities/2016/apr/30/housing-crisis -poll-city-country-split-blame).

## A NOTE ON THE LONGLIST

We have selected seven of the longlisted essays which are especially worthy of mention.

In her essay 'Axe the property tax: how to end Whitehall's reign on the housing market and restore homeowner sovereignty', Sharni Cutajar discusses the role of property taxes in decreasing household liquidity and homeowner mobility, in particular the Stamp Duty Land Tax (SDLT) imposed on the sale and acquisition of property, and the Capital Gains Tax (CGT) imposed on assets such as investment property. These both create inefficient allocations and dramatic welfare losses on society, limiting productivity and dynamism in cities where the cost of living becomes too high. 'Prosperity and progress' by Jacob Waldock addresses the existing property taxes of Council Tax and Business Rates in an essay exploring the role of more efficient land use in rejuvenating the housing market, while in 'Market Liberation Act' Rohan Chaturvedi proposes both deregulation and tax cuts as means of increasing the supply of new housing.

Jamie Parker's 'Incentivising the housing market' finds that if a larger proportion of the benefits of housebuilding were transferred to local authorities through fiscal devolution, then new developments would be more welcome. The great macroeconomic reformers in the 1980s understood how aligning structural incentives can have powerful dynamic effects that drive the whole economy. 'Planning devolution' by Usama Safeer reminds us that we should target market-distorting regulations and provide an alternative to our dysfunctional planning system. Devolving the planning system will also mean competition between subnational levels of government, creating a 'market' in policy. But this needs the support of a decentralised fiscal system, rewarding development with fiscal benefits such as better public services, lower tax rates, or both. Bethany Bloomer's 'Tax land, not houses' also looks at this question.

Finally, in 'Your property – liberalising land and giving people the power to free themselves by building a market for planning rights', Angus Groom analyses the capacity of 'decentralised bargaining' to bring together developers and local communities, demonstrating that so-called Nimbys do not generally object to new housing per se, but do not want new houses without proper infrastructure, for example. Bargaining could better allow developers to provide the local community with the things they value.

# ABOUT THE IEA

The Institute is a research and educational charity (No. CC 235 351), limited by guarantee. Its mission is to improve understanding of the fundamental institutions of a free society by analysing and expounding the role of markets in solving economic and social problems.

The IEA achieves its mission by:

- a high-quality publishing programme
- conferences, seminars, lectures and other events
- outreach to school and college students
- brokering media introductions and appearances

The IEA, which was established in 1955 by the late Sir Antony Fisher, is an educational charity, not a political organisation. It is independent of any political party or group and does not carry on activities intended to affect support for any political party or candidate in any election or referendum, or at any other time. It is financed by sales of publications, conference fees and voluntary donations.

In addition to its main series of publications, the IEA also publishes (jointly with the University of Buckingham), *Economic Affairs*.

The IEA is aided in its work by a distinguished international Academic Advisory Council and an eminent panel of Honorary Fellows. Together with other academics, they review prospective IEA publications, their comments being passed on anonymously to authors. All IEA papers are therefore subject to the same rigorous independent refereeing process as used by leading academic journals.

IEA publications enjoy widespread classroom use and course adoptions in schools and universities. They are also sold throughout the world and often translated/reprinted.

Since 1974 the IEA has helped to create a worldwide network of 100 similar institutions in over 70 countries. They are all independent but share the IEA's mission.

Views expressed in the IEA's publications are those of the authors, not those of the Institute (which has no corporate view), its Managing Trustees, Academic Advisory Council members or senior staff.

Members of the Institute's Academic Advisory Council, Honorary Fellows, Trustees and Staff are listed on the following page.

---

The Institute gratefully acknowledges financial support for its publications programme and other work from a generous benefaction by the late Professor Ronald Coase.

Other books recently published by the IEA include:

*Forever Contemporary: The Economics of Ronald Coase*
Edited by Cento Veljanovski
Readings in Political Economy 4; ISBN 978-0-255-36710-3; £15.00

*Power Cut? How the EU Is Pulling the Plug on Electricity Markets*
Carlo Stagnaro
Hobart Paperback 180; ISBN 978-0-255-36716-5; £10.00

*Policy Stability and Economic Growth – Lessons from the Great Recession*
John B. Taylor
Readings in Political Economy 5; ISBN 978-0-255-36719-6; £7.50

*Breaking Up Is Hard To Do: Britain and Europe's Dysfunctional Relationship*
Edited by Patrick Minford and J. R. Shackleton
Hobart Paperback 181; ISBN 978-0-255-36722-6; £15.00

*In Focus: The Case for Privatising the BBC*
Edited by Philip Booth
Hobart Paperback 182; ISBN 978-0-255-36725-7; £12.50

*Islamic Foundations of a Free Society*
Edited by Nouh El Harmouzi and Linda Whetstone
Hobart Paperback 183; ISBN 978-0-255-36728-8; £12.50

*The Economics of International Development: Foreign Aid versus Freedom for the World's Poor*
William Easterly
Readings in Political Economy 6; ISBN 978-0-255-36731-8; £7.50

*Taxation, Government Spending and Economic Growth*
Edited by Philip Booth
Hobart Paperback 184; ISBN 978-0-255-36734-9; £15.00

*Universal Healthcare without the NHS: Towards a Patient-Centred Health System*
Kristian Niemietz
Hobart Paperback 185; ISBN 978-0-255-36737-0; £10.00

*Sea Change: How Markets and Property Rights Could Transform the Fishing Industry*
Edited by Richard Wellings
Readings in Political Economy 7; ISBN 978-0-255-36740-0; £10.00

*Working to Rule: The Damaging Economics of UK Employment Regulation*
J. R. Shackleton
Hobart Paperback 186; ISBN 978-0-255-36743-1; £15.00

*Education, War and Peace: The Surprising Success of Private Schools in War-Torn Countries*
James Tooley and David Longfield
ISBN 978-0-255-36746-2; £10.00

*Killjoys: A Critique of Paternalism*
Christopher Snowdon
ISBN 978-0-255-36749-3; £12.50

*Financial Stability without Central Banks*
George Selgin, Kevin Dowd and Mathieu Bédard
ISBN 978-0-255-36752-3; £10.00

*Against the Grain: Insights from an Economic Contrarian*
Paul Ormerod
ISBN 978-0-255-36755-4; £15.00

*Ayn Rand: An Introduction*
Eamonn Butler
ISBN 978-0-255-36764-6; £12.50

*Capitalism: An Introduction*
Eamonn Butler
ISBN 978-0-255-36758-5; £12.50

*Opting Out: Conscience and Cooperation in a Pluralistic Society*
David S. Oderberg
ISBN 978-0-255-36761-5; £12.50

*Getting the Measure of Money: A Critical Assessment of UK Monetary Indicators*
Anthony J. Evans
ISBN 978-0-255-36767-7; £12.50

*Socialism: The Failed Idea That Never Dies*
Kristian Niemietz
ISBN 978-0-255-36770-7; £17.50

*Top Dogs and Fat Cats: The Debate on High Pay*
Edited by J. R. Shackleton
ISBN 978-0-255-36773-8; £15.00

*School Choice around the World … And the Lessons We Can Learn*
Edited by Pauline Dixon and Steve Humble
ISBN 978-0-255-36779-0; £15.00

*School of Thought: 101 Great Liberal Thinkers*
Eamonn Butler
ISBN 978-0-255-36776-9; £12.50

## Other IEA publications

Comprehensive information on other publications and the wider work of the IEA can be found at www.iea.org.uk. To order any publication please see below.

## Personal customers

Orders from personal customers should be directed to the IEA:

Clare Rusbridge
IEA
2 Lord North Street
FREEPOST LON10168
London SW1P 3YZ
Tel: 020 7799 8907. Fax: 020 7799 2137
Email: sales@iea.org.uk

## Trade customers

All orders from the book trade should be directed to the IEA's distributor:

NBN International (IEA Orders)
Orders Dept.
NBN International
10 Thornbury Road
Plymouth PL6 7PP
Tel: 01752 202301, Fax: 01752 202333
Email: orders@nbninternational.com

## IEA subscriptions

The IEA also offers a subscription service to its publications. For a single annual payment (currently £42.00 in the UK), subscribers receive every monograph the IEA publishes. For more information please contact:

Clare Rusbridge
Subscriptions
IEA
2 Lord North Street
FREEPOST LON10168
London SW1P 3YZ
Tel: 020 7799 8907, Fax: 020 7799 2137
Email: crusbridge@iea.org.uk